970.004   Lacey, Theresa Jensen
Lac

The Pawnee

THE
PAWNEE

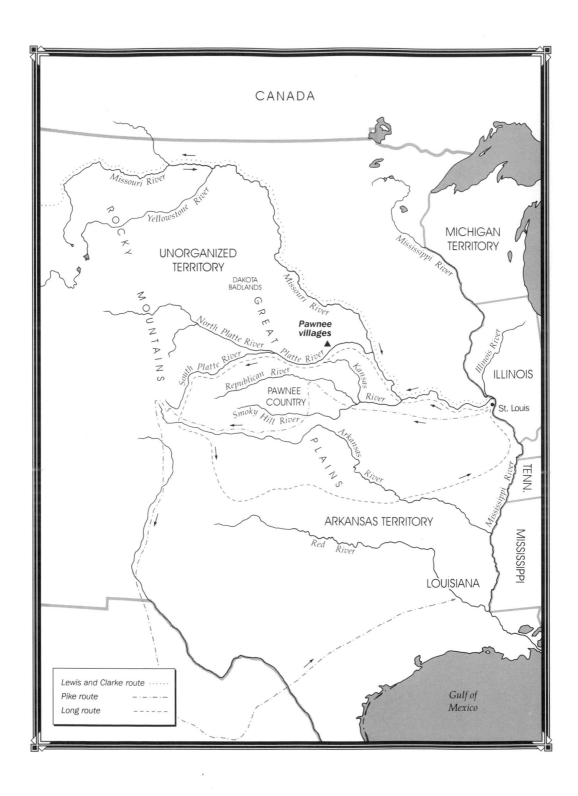

CANADA

MICHIGAN
TERRITORY

Mississippi River

Missouri River

Yellowstone River

ROCKY

UNORGANIZED
TERRITORY

DAKOTA
BADLANDS

Missouri River

**Pawnee
villages**

MOUNTAINS

GREAT

North Platte River

Platte River

South Platte River

Republican River

PAWNEE
COUNTRY

*Kansas
River*

Smoky Hill River

PLAINS

*Arkansas
River*

ILLINOIS

Illinois River

St. Louis

TENN.

Mississippi River

MISSISSIPPI

ARKANSAS TERRITORY

Red River

LOUISIANA

Lewis and Clarke route ....
Pike route _._._._
Long route _ _ _ _

*Gulf of
Mexico*

THE PAWNEE

Theresa Jensen Lacey

Frank W. Porter III
General Editor

CHELSEA HOUSE PUBLISHERS

New York   Philadelphia

On the cover A Pawnee drum from the 1890s, used in part of a Ghost Dance ceremony.

Chelsea House Publishers
Editorial Director Richard Rennert
Executive Managing Editor Karyn Gullen Browne
Copy Chief Robin James
Picture Editor Adrian G. Allen
Creative Director Robert Mitchell
Art Director Joan Ferrigno
Production Manager Sallye Scott

Indians of North America
Senior Editor Sean Dolan
Native American Specialist Jack Miller

Staff for **THE PAWNEE**
Associate Editor Mary B. Sisson
Senior Designer Cambraia Magalhães
Picture Researcher Sandy Jones

First Printing
1 3 5 7 9 8 6 4 2

Library of Congress Cataloging-in-Publication Data
Lacey, Theresa Jensen.
    The Pawnee / Theresa Jensen Lacey; Frank W. Porter III, general editor.
        p. cm. — (Indians of North America)
    Includes bibliographical references and index.
    Summary: Examines the history, culture, changing fortunes, and current situation of the Pawnee Indians.
    ISBN 0-7910-1683-8
          0-7910-3481-X (pbk.)
    1. Pawnee Indians. [1. Pawnee Indians. 2. Indians of North America—Great Plains.] I. Porter, Frank W., 1947- .
II. Title. III. Series: Indians of North America (Chelsea House Publishers)
E99.P3L33 1995   95-15814
970.004'979—dc20   CIP
                                                    AC

CONTENTS

INDIANS OF NORTH AMERICA

CHELSEA HOUSE PUBLISHERS

INDIANS OF NORTH AMERICA: CONFLICT AND SURVIVAL

Frank W. Porter III

> *The Indians survived our open intention of wiping them out, and since the tide turned they have even weathered our good intentions toward them, which can be much more deadly.*
>
> John Steinbeck
> *America and Americans*

When Europeans first reached the North American continent, they found hundreds of tribes occupying a vast and rich country. The newcomers quickly recognized the wealth of natural resources. They were not, however, so quick or willing to recognize the spiritual, cultural, and intellectual riches of the people they called Indians.

The Indians of North America examines the problems that develop when people with different cultures come together. For American Indians, the consequences of their interaction with non-Indian people have been both productive and tragic. The Europeans believed they had "discovered" a "New World," but their religious bigotry, cultural bias, and materialistic world view kept them from appreciating and understanding the people who lived in it. All too often they attempted to change the way of life of the indigenous people. The Spanish conquistadores wanted the Indians as a source of labor. The Christian missionaries, many of whom were English, viewed them as potential converts. French traders and trappers used the Indians as a means to obtain pelts. As Francis Parkman, the 19th-century historian, stated, "Spanish civilization crushed the Indian; English civilization scorned and neglected him. French civilization embraced and cherished him."

Nearly 500 years later, many people think of American Indians as curious vestiges of a distant past, waging a futile war to survive in a Space Age society. Even today, our understanding of the history and culture of American Indians is too often derived from unsympathetic, culturally biased, and inaccurate reports. The American Indian, described and portrayed in thousands of movies, television programs, books, articles, and government studies, has either been raised to the status of the "noble savage" or disparaged as the "wild Indian" who resisted the westward expansion of the American frontier.

Where in this popular view are the real Indians, the human beings and communities whose ancestors can be traced back to ice-age hunters? Where are the creative and indomitable people whose sophisticated technologies used the natural resources to ensure their survival, whose military skill might even have prevented European settlement of North America if not for devastating epidemics and disruption of the ecology? Where are the men and women who are today diligently struggling to assert their legal rights and express once again the value of their heritage?

The various Indian tribes of North America, like people everywhere, have a history that includes population expansion, adaptation to a range of regional environments, trade across wide networks, internal strife, and warfare. This was the reality. Europeans justified their conquests, however, by creating a mythical image of the New World and its native people. In this myth, the New World was a virgin land, waiting for the Europeans. The arrival of Christopher Columbus ended a timeless primitiveness for the original inhabitants.

Also part of this myth was the debate over the origins of the American Indians. Fantastic and diverse answers were proposed by the early explorers, missionaries, and settlers. Some thought that the Indians were descended from the Ten Lost Tribes of Israel, others that they were descended from inhabitants of the lost continent of Atlantis. One writer suggested that the Indians had reached North America in another Noah's ark.

A later myth, perpetrated by many historians, focused on the relentless persecution during the past five centuries until only a scattering of these "primitive" people remained to be herded onto reservations. This view fails to chronicle the overt and covert ways in which the Indians successfully coped with the intruders.

All of these myths presented one-sided interpretations that ignored the complexity of European and American events and policies. All left serious questions unanswered. What were the origins of the American Indians? Where did they come from? How and when did they get to the New World? What was their life—their culture—really like?

In the late 1800s, anthropologists and archaeologists in the Smithsonian Institution's newly created Bureau of American Ethnology in Washington,

D.C., began to study scientifically the history and culture of the Indians of North America. They were motivated by an honest belief that the Indians were on the verge of extinction and that along with them would vanish their languages, religious beliefs, technology, myths, and legends. These men and women went out to visit, study, and record data from as many Indian communities as possible before this information was forever lost.

By this time there was a new myth in the national consciousness. American Indians existed as figures in the American past. They had performed a historical mission. They had challenged white settlers who trekked across the continent. Once conquered, however, they were supposed to accept graciously the way of life of their conquerors.

The reality again was different. American Indians resisted both actively and passively. They refused to lose their unique identity, to be assimilated into white society. Many whites viewed the Indians not only as members of a conquered nation but also as "inferior" and "unequal." The rights of the Indians could be expanded, contracted, or modified as the conquerors saw fit. In every generation, white society asked itself what to do with the American Indians. Their answers have resulted in the twists and turns of federal Indian policy.

There were two general approaches. One way was to raise the Indians to a "higher level" by "civilizing" them. Zealous missionaries considered it their Christian duty to elevate the Indian through conversion and scanty education. The other approach was to ignore the Indians until they disappeared under pressure from the ever-expanding white society. The myth of the "vanishing Indian" gave stronger support to the latter option, helping to justify the taking of the Indians' land.

Prior to the end of the 18th century, there was no national policy on Indians simply because the American nation had not yet come into existence. American Indians similarly did not possess a political or social unity with which to confront the various Europeans. They were not homogeneous. Rather, they were loosely formed bands and tribes, speaking nearly 300 languages and thousands of dialects. The collective identity felt by Indians today is a result of their common experiences of defeat and/or mistreatment at the hands of whites.

During the colonial period, the British crown did not have a coordinated policy toward the Indians of North America. Specific tribes (most notably the Iroquois and the Cherokee) became military and political pawns used by both the crown and the individual colonies. The success of the American Revolution brought no immediate change. When the United States acquired new territory from France and Mexico in the early 19th century, the federal government wanted to open this land to settlement by homesteaders. But the Indian tribes that lived on this land had signed treaties with European governments assuring their title to the land. Now the United States assumed legal responsibility for honoring these treaties.

At first, President Thomas Jefferson believed that the Louisiana Purchase contained sufficient land for both the Indians and the white population. Within a generation, though, it became clear that the Indians would not be allowed to remain. In the 1830s the federal government began to coerce the eastern tribes to sign treaties agreeing to relinquish their ancestral land and move west of the Mississippi River. Whenever these negotiations failed, President Andrew Jackson used the military to remove the Indians. The southeastern tribes, promised food and transportation during their removal to the West, were instead forced to walk the "Trail of Tears." More than 4,000 men, woman, and children died during this forced march. The "removal policy" was successful in opening the land to homesteaders, but it created enormous hardships for the Indians.

By 1871 most of the tribes in the United States had signed treaties ceding most or all of their ancestral land in exchange for reservations and welfare. The treaty terms were intended to bind both parties for all time. But in the General Allotment Act of 1887, the federal government changed its policy again. Now the goal was to make tribal members into individual landowners and farmers, encouraging their absorption into white society. This policy was advantageous to whites who were eager to acquire Indian land, but it proved disastrous for the Indians. One hundred thirty-eight million acres of reservation land were subdivided into tracts of 160, 80, or as little as 40 acres, and allotted tribe members on an individual basis. Land owned in this way was said to have "trust status" and could not be sold. But the surplus land— all Indian land not allotted to individuals—was opened (for sale) to white settlers. Ultimately, more than 90 million acres of land were taken from the Indians by legal and illegal means.

The resulting loss of land was a catastrophe for the Indians. It was necessary to make it illegal for Indians to sell their land to non-Indians. The Indian Reorganization Act of 1934 officially ended the allotment period. Tribes that voted to accept the provisions of this act were reorganized, and an effort was made to purchase land within preexisting reservations to restore an adequate land base.

Ten years later, in 1944, federal Indian policy again shifted. Now the federal government wanted to get out of the "Indian business." In 1953 an act of Congress named specific tribes whose trust status was to be ended "at the earliest possible time." This new law enabled the United States to end unilaterally, whether the Indians wished it or not, the special status that protected the land in Indian tribal reservations. In the 1950s federal Indian policy was to transfer federal responsibility and jurisdiction to state governments, encourage the physical relocation of Indian peoples from reservations to urban areas, and hasten the termination, or extinction, of tribes.

Between 1954 and 1962 Congress passed specific laws authorizing the termination of more than 100 tribal groups. The stated purpose of the termination policy was to ensure the full and complete integration of Indians into American society. However, there is a less benign way to interpret this legislation. Even as termination was being discussed in Congress, 133 separate bills were introduced to permit the transfer of trust land ownership from Indians to non-Indians.

With the Johnson administration in the 1960s the federal government began to reject termination. In the 1970s yet another Indian policy emerged. Known as "self-determination," it favored keeping the protective role of the federal government while increasing tribal participation in, and control of, important areas of local government. In 1983 President Reagan, in a policy statement on Indian affairs, restated the unique "government is government" relationship of the United States with the Indians. However, federal programs since then have moved toward transferring Indian affairs to individual states, which have long desired to gain control of Indian land and resources.

As long as American Indians retain power, land, and resources that are coveted by the states and the federal government, there will continue to be a "clash of cultures," and the issues will be contested in the courts, Congress, the White House, and even in the international human rights community. To give all Americans a greater comprehension of the issues and conflicts involving American Indians today is a major goal of this series. These issues are not easily understood, nor can these conflicts be readily resolved. The study of North American Indian history and culture is a necessary and important step toward that comprehension. All Americans must learn the history of the relations between the Indians and the federal government, recognize the unique legal status of the Indians, and understand the heritage and cultures of the Indians of North America.

Walking Sun was a Pawnee medicine man. The tribe's name was derived from a word referring to the stiffened, upraised tufts of hair that many Pawnee men wore.

ORIGINS
OF
THE
PAWNEE

The prairie lands in which the Pawnee settled, known to the European immigrants as the Nebraska Territory, was one from which they had a grand view of the night skies. It was natural for their beliefs in the beginnings of life to center around the stars. The heavens provided the Pawnee with a basis for their religion, directed their lives, and fueled their imaginations. The stars also served as inspiration for their creation myth.

The Pawnee god from which all life sprang has been referred to as *Atius Tirawa,* or *Tirawahat,* or simply *Tirawa,* which means "The Expanse of the Heavens." The Pawnee say that there was always Tirawa; in the beginning, there was only Tirawa. Tirawa lived in the heavens. He was alone, and wanted something or someone else for company. But before he did anything about it, he stopped to think about what he wanted to do. It is important to note that thought before action is intrinsic to the Pawnee philosophy of life. To the Pawnee, there can be nothing without there first being thought. The thinking individual was the very essence of humanity, the connection with the Great Mind.

Therefore the process of creation began with Tirawa having thoughts about it. He decided he would like to have a universe and stars and so created the first ones, placing them in the four cardinal directions. The Evening Star was placed in the west; she was given the moon to help her. In the east, Tirawa placed the Morning Star; he was given the sun as his helper. In the other two cardinal directions he placed the North Star and the South Star. Tirawa also placed four stars in the semicardinal directions (the northeast, northwest, southeast, and southwest), and told them that they were to hold the heavens up for all eternity.

The stars in the four cardinal directions were given the power to create the earth. Tirawa gave the Evening Star tools with which to do this. She was given all the ingredients she would need to make life-giving storms: wind, clouds, lightning, and thunder.

Evening Star caused the first storm. With one great flash of lightning, a loud clap of thunder, and a fierce wind, the earth was created; but there was no life on it or in it. Tirawa told the Evening Star to sing; when she did, the face of the earth became covered with water.

Tirawa told the stars in the four semicardinal directions to strike the earth with war clubs made of hemlock. When they did, the waters parted; dry land and mountains appeared. Another storm came, the wind blew, the rain fell hard upon the earth, and lightning struck the ground. The lightning made the earth fertile and able to sustain life. Thunder shook the ground; as it settled from the shaking, the earth formed mountains and valleys. Another storm came, and the forests and other fauna were created. A fourth storm caused rains to come to earth, filling the shallow places of the land with sweet, fresh water.

The star-gods then dropped seeds upon the earth. The seeds sprouted and became living plants. After this, Tirawa rested for a time.

Tirawa told the stars, "Take human form; make people on the earth in that image." But in a council with the other

The hairstyle exhibited by this Pawnee warrior was even more characteristic of the tonsorial fashion that gave the tribe the name it was called by outsiders.

stars, Morning Star and Evening Star quarreled. Morning Star was in love with Evening Star and knew that they should have children. Morning Star knew that this was the only way the earth would ever have people on it, and he was determined to have Evening Star as his wife. Up in the sky, knowing that Morning Star was coming for her, Evening Star put four fierce animals in the semicardinal directions. She put a wolf in the southeast and gave him the power of clouds. In the southwest, Evening Star placed a wildcat, who had the power of the winds. She placed a mountain lion in the northwest, and gave him the power of lightning. In the northeast, Evening Star placed a bear with the power of thunder. She said, "When Morning Star comes, you are all to attack him."

Before Morning Star came, other stars tried to court Evening Star; she had her animals dispatch them all. But Morning Star had help in the form of the Sun. When finally Morning Star and the Sun came for her, Evening Star and her guard animals had been fighting off all other would-be suitors. Seeing Morning Star with the Sun, Evening Star and her guard animals were taken aback. She said, "You have been brave and determined. I believe you are worthy of me now." Evening Star agreed to marry Morning Star. Together they made the very first human being, a female child. She was carried from heaven to earth by a whirlwind. Later, Evening Star and Morning Star had another child, a male. He was also sent to earth.

The population of the earth increased over time. Evening Star instructed the females in the care of the earth's gifts, how to make a tipi and an earth lodge, and how to care for chil-

dren. The male children were taught by Morning Star how to protect themselves and their families, how to hunt, and how to travel over the earth. Morning Star gave the male children their warrior's clothing. Evening Star came many times to see how her children fared, and she taught the people sacred songs and the stories of creation so that they would always remember.

After a while, the people went out hunting, farther and farther from their camp, until they came upon other people; then they knew that they were not the only ones on earth. There were many people on the face of the earth, much like themselves, only a little different.

The first boy child made by Morning Star and Evening Star grew up and was called the First Man. After discovering these other villages, First Man sent messengers to them, inviting them to a great council. He moved his village to a more centralized location, so it would be convenient for all of the people to meet. This village became known as Center Village; First Man was called Chief of Center Village.

The people of the other villages came to the council, bearing gifts and buffalo meat. So that each village would know it had equal responsibilities toward the people and could enjoy as much regard as any other, Chief of Center Village created different medicine bundles, or a collection of sacred things, for each of them. With the help of Evening Star and Morning Star, Chief of Center Village and all the peo-

The Platte River flowed right through the heart of Pawnee territory. Wide but very shallow, the Platte waters a surrounding flat valley that was a natural route west for pioneers as well as for the first transcontinental railroad.

ple developed their ceremonies, symbols, and special songs. It was then that the people banded together to form a nation, bound with the spiritual gifts they shared.

The establishing of ceremonies gave order to the cycles of Pawnee life and coordinated their actions, giving meaning to the smallest things they did. Even today, in the cycle of season-

not only around the stars but around the animals that were part of their environment. One of the animals that figures prominently in legend is the sandhill crane. Every spring for thousands of years, sandhill cranes have come in great numbers to the sandbars of the Platte River. Here they rest and feed on marsh tubers and small reptiles, gaining strength and weight for the long flight to their Arctic nesting grounds. Seeing these birds every spring, the Pawnee were both mystified and fascinated by them, with their large bodies, long necks, and loud, trumpeting calls. There are some stories in which the cranes cause mischief and bring trouble for the people; this is such a story.

One very hot summer night, many of the people came out of their tipis to sleep under the open sky, with the cool breezes and the sweet smell of the prairie grasses blowing over them. Among them was a young girl named Feather Woman. Just before dawn, Feather Woman awoke suddenly and looked up into the sky, which was still dark. She watched the bright Morning Star as it rose and was fascinated. Feather Woman whispered, "Morning Star, I love you! If I could find a husband who is as beautiful as you, I would be happy." She watched the Morning Star until it faded with the rising of the sun.

That summer, Feather Woman and her people were very busy. The buffalo were plentiful; many had been brought down in the hunt. There was

al ceremonies, the people use medicine bundles. There is an Evening Star bundle, representing the creation; a Morning Star bundle; bundles representing the four semicardinal directions; and the Skull bundle, which represents intellectual creativity, especially as it came from the First Man.

Many of the beliefs in the legends and old stories of the Pawnee centered much to be done: animals to skin, meat to cook and preserve, clothing and tools to craft. With so much to occupy her, Feather Woman had little time to think about the Morning Star.

Then, one fall afternoon, Feather Woman went out to look for firewood. So intent was she on her work, she wandered far from her people. After a time she sensed someone watching her. Turning, she gazed upon a very tall, handsome young warrior she had never seen before. The stranger was dressed in a soft white buckskin robe, beautifully embroidered and decorated with dyed porcupine quills. In his hair he wore eagle feathers; in his hand he carried a small juniper bush decorated with cobwebs.

Apprehensive, Feather Woman started to run away. The stranger caught her arm and whispered, "Feather Woman! I am Morning Star! One night last summer, I looked down; I saw you lying there in the prairie grasses, waking up beside your tipi. I fell in love with you. I heard you say that you loved me. Forget your people and come with me now! I will take you to my country, the land of the Star People."

Feather Woman hesitated, but only for an instant. She nodded, and Morning Star laid the juniper bush on the ground. He said, "Put your feet on the lowest strand of cobwebs and close your eyes." With this, Feather Woman was swept up into the sky. She opened her eyes in Star Country, with Morning Star by her side. She discovered that Star Country was much like her own, with grassy plains, hills, and lodges. Morning Star explained, "Spider Man weaves the cobwebs; we use them as ladders to come down to earth and then to return again to the sky." He then took Feather Woman to his own lodge, also the home of his parents, Sun and Moon.

Sun was out, but Moon was at home. She was very kind to Feather Woman, but she took her son aside and said, "Morning Star, your father will not like this marriage. He does not trust earth people. Tell Feather Woman to be wary of this, because if she disobeys any of our laws, Sun will banish her from Star Country."

Just as Moon had said, when Sun came to the lodge that night, he was indeed unhappy to meet the wife Morning Star had chosen. Sun said, "Earth people are weak and stupid. They can't be trusted." But then he said to Feather Woman, "If you obey our laws and learn our way of life, you can stay and you will be happy."

Some seasons later, Feather Woman had a child. Morning Star named him Star Boy. They were all very happy, until one day when Feather Woman went with Moon to get roots and berries. In their wanderings, they came upon a huge turnip, larger than any Feather Woman had ever seen before. The green leaves were almost as tall as she was, and the turnip was only half-buried in the earth. She was tempted to dig it up, for what a great meal it would make.

A Pawnee village along the Platte, as painted by the American artist George Catlin, who spent most of the 1830s traveling among and painting the Indians of the Great Plains. Some of the earliest visual documentations of the Pawnee are paintings done by artists who visited the American West, such as Catlin, Charles Bird King, and Karl Bodmer.

Moon said, "I see you looking at that turnip, Feather Woman. It is sacred to the Star People. Underneath the turnip lies a secret we are forbidden to know. Whoever tries to disturb this turnip will bring great sadness upon themselves. Never touch it!" Several days passed, and whenever Moon and Feather Woman would be out digging for roots or gathering firewood, they would pass the turnip.

Feather Woman's digging stick itched in her hand, but she did not want to anger Moon and so refrained from giving in to temptation.

One day, however, Moon said to Feather Woman, "I must stay here in our lodge today; I feel unwell. You go on without me." And so she did. After a while, her gathering brought her close to where the great turnip lay. She said to herself, "No one will know. I will only uproot it a little and see what lies underneath, and then bury it again." She began to dig; as she did, two cranes swooped down from the sky and said to her, "We will help you uproot that turnip with our beaks!" Feather Woman was glad for their help; she did not know that the cranes were enemies of the Star People.

The cranes smiled maliciously as they flew away, leaving the great turnip uprooted and lying on its side. "There!" they called out to Feather Woman. "Now see what lies beneath!" Trumpeting loudly, they flew away. There was a huge crater where the turnip had been. Feather Woman looked down into it, and far below she could see her former home. She saw some of her friends gathering berries

The renowned photographer William Henry Jackson took this 1868 photograph of a Pawnee painting on buffalo hide, which records events from the tribe's past. Buffalo and horses were both crucially important in Pawnee culture.

on a hillside, and some of the warriors gathered around a fine horse one of them had just brought to camp. Feather Woman saw the children beside the fires, and the women shooing them away as they cooked. And suddenly, she was overwhelmed with a feeling of great longing for her former home and for her people.

Feather Woman watched her people through the crater, until she realized that darkness was falling. She rolled the turnip back to its place and tried to rebury it as best she could. It had been dark for a long time when she returned to her lodge; she had been missed. Once there, Sun saw her face and said, "Feather Woman, you look sad and also guilty, as if you have done something wrong. Tell me what it is!" Then Feather Woman told Sun what she had done.

"I knew that we could not trust earth people," Sun said to Moon and Morning Star. To Feather Woman he said, "You have betrayed our trust and disturbed something that is sacred to us. You must be banished, and you will go back to the earth-home you so much long for."

Morning Star led Feather Woman and her son, Star Boy, to the place where Spider Man wove his cobwebs. Morning Star wrapped them in a white buckskin robe. Spider Man tied her with his cobwebs and led her down from the sky. As she came down, her earth people looked up in the heavens, saying, "Look! It is a great falling star!" They watched its brightness all the

The Evening Star medicine bundle of the Pawnee. The Pawnee believed that the first human beings were born of the union between the Evening Star and the Morning Star, and it was the Evening Star who taught them how to look after the land, to build lodgings, and to care for children.

way to earth. Then they went to look for the star, to see where it had fallen.

There they found Star Boy and Feather Woman, wrapped in the white robe. They were unhurt. The people took Feather Woman and Star Boy back to their camp, for they remembered her from former days.

But Feather Woman never stopped grieving for her love, the Morning Star.

Archaeologists in present-day Nebraska uncovered the remains of this earth lodge that had been made by the Pawnee's prehistoric ancestors. They believe that what is shown here was the lodge's central firepit.

Every night, she would climb the highest hill and watch the skies until Morning Star appeared. She would call out, "Morning Star! Please take me back with you!" And he would respond, "You betrayed our trust; you can never return." And he would go on his way across the sky. Feather Woman finally died of a broken heart. Morning Star can still be seen each clear dawn, crossing the sky, alone.

Another popular Pawnee myth is the legend of Bear-Man. One day a young warrior on a horse raid saw a female bear cub alone in the forest. The cub looked so defenseless and small that the brave was moved with sympathy for her. He took the cub in his arms and said, "I know that our Great Spirit, Tirawa, will care for you; but I will tie a string of tobacco around your neck, to show you that I, too, care." With that, he gently knotted a tobacco string around the cub's neck and put her down again.

Once back in his lodge, the young man told his wife, who was soon to have a baby, about the bear cub. She thought so much about this bear cub that when their child was born, he looked much like a cub himself.

As the child grew older, he became more and more like a bear, both in his looks and in his ways. Even as the boy played with his friends, he would tell them, "I can turn myself into a real bear whenever I want to." They, of course, did not believe him. Still, the young boy was given a certain amount of respect by his people, for among the Pawnee the bear is considered to be the wisest of all animals.

As the boy grew older, he was asked to accompany war and raiding parties, to lend his wisdom to them. One fateful day, however, when he was with over 40 Pawnee warriors, they were set upon by a large band of Sioux, a tribe considered to be one of their greatest enemies. The Sioux killed the Pawnees, including Bear-Man, and took their scalps. Shortly afterward, some bears wandered by the ravine where the ambush had happened. A she-bear recognized Bear-Man as the child of the kind man who had blessed her with his tobacco string, long ago; and she implored of her friends, "Let us use our medicine to make Bear-Man live again." And so together they sang the special songs and used the healing herbs about which they all knew. After a time, Bear-Man began to stir with life once more.

When Bear-Man became conscious, the bears took him to their den to fully recover and told him what they had done. As he healed, the bears taught Bear-Man even more about good medicines and all the other wise things they knew. They said, "When you use these powers, thank not ourselves, nor think that you do this by your own powers; instead, in all things give thanks to Tirawa, who made us and gave us our wisdom." They told Bear-Man, "You must go back to your people now, with all you have learned. The cedar tree shall be a protector to you in all that you do, because it never ages. If, during one of Tirawa's thunderstorms, you throw some cedar wood upon your fire, it will keep you safe." The bears blessed Bear-Man with their wisdom, greatness, and fearlessness.

Bear-Man returned to his people, teaching them all that the bears had taught him. He became the greatest warrior of his tribe; he was fearless, wise, and great, just as the bears had said. Bear-Man lived long ago, but such was his influence with his people that there is a special dance they made in his memory. It is called the Bear Dance, and the Pawnee still dance the Bear Dance and remember their source of wisdom, fearlessness, and greatness.

Mythology aside, historical accounts of the origin of the Pawnee refer to their ancestors, the Caddoans. The Caddoan peoples' history has been dated to prehistoric times. These tribes included the Wichita, the Arikara, the Caddo, and the Pawnee. Besides sharing linguistic similarities, these tribes also had similar lifestyles, hunting and cultivation methods, and types of dwelling.

There are a number of theories of how the Caddoans came to be on the North American continent. A four-tribal-origin theory has been borne out by researchers and geneticists, who have identified four distinct DNA strains from the various tribes and hypothetically traced the migratory paths of each. Other anthropologists say that some Native American peoples came to this continent by ocean passage, crossing the Pacific and Atlantic.

Although no one can say for certain, the most popular and commonly accepted theory is that all Native American peoples traveled to this continent from Asia over 40,000 years ago, utilizing a small strip of treeless land then in existence, a "land bridge" joining the two continents at the juncture of Siberia and Alaska, at the site of what is now known as the Bering Strait.

The Caddoans, the ancestors of the Pawnee, lived and prospered in the fertile lands west of the Mississippi River. As time passed and tribal populations grew, they began traveling farther away in search of game. Their travels took them to the territory that has become Nebraska and Kansas.

These lands were occupied by several Native American peoples, including the Pawnee, the Caddoans, and the Kansa Indians. It is a land of rolling hills and vast prairies, with bitterly cold weather and sudden snowstorms in winter; dry, hot days in summer; and flash floods in spring. The Kansas and Arkansas rivers, with over 100 tributaries, brought life-giving water to the people, as well as an abundance of game and wildlife.

The land that we now know as Nebraska must have been a beautiful sight to the early Native American people, with its undulating plains, fertile soil, rugged hills called buttes, and over 2,000 lakes. The majority of the Pawnee population settled along the Platte River, a tributary of the Missouri. Nebraska, like Kansas, is also a land of unpredictable and extreme weather. This environment challenged the Pawnee in their daily struggle for survival and enriched them spiritually as a people.

The lands of Kansas and Nebraska were shared by the Pawnee with neighboring tribes, some of which were friends, some trading partners, and others bitter foes. Certain neighboring tribes, such as the Blackfeet, Arapaho, Kiowa, and Apache, were in the Plains area as early as 500 B.C. The Pawnee migrated to the Plains from the southwestern part of the continent about 700 years ago, or approximately A.D. 1250.

Perhaps they settled in that area because of the lure of abundant game, especially buffalo. Another contributing factor was trade. The Plains area was the connecting hub of an ancient intertribal trade route, so goods could be obtained even from tribes with whom the Pawnee were unfriendly.

Photographed in the 1860s, the Pawnee leader Eagle Chief displays many of the items of apparel and everyday use that characterized Pawnee culture by that time.

For the Pawnee, as for other Native American peoples, even objects of everyday use reflected the tribe's spiritual concerns. The star design on the drum at upper left, for example, was a common motif in Pawnee decoration that emphasized the importance of the heavens in Pawnee belief.

The Pawnee might have traveled farther east, but soon after they arrived they encountered an influx of other tribes from the east fleeing the invasion of white settlers in their former lands. Eastern woodlands tribes such as the Sioux arrived, being forced ever westward by more and more European settlers. Ahead of the Sioux came the Cheyenne and Crow, who were also forced out of the east. After the Plains tribes had acquired the horse from the Spanish, however, each tribe began to stand their ground and defend lands they claimed as their own.

By the mid–18th century, five principal tribes had established themselves in the area. North of where the Kansas and Missouri rivers met was the tribe that gave Kansas its name—the Kansa, or Kaw. South of them were the Osage. Both of these tribes had come from the east. The Pawnee claimed the entire north-central portion of the Plains as their own, with the Wichita tribe to the south. Arriving from the eastern Rockies, the Comanches lived in what is now western Kansas.

The Plains area the Pawnee people chose to call home ranged from the northern headwaters of the Platte River, through the Republican, Solomon, and Smoky Hill valleys, then farther south through the Great Bend of the Arkansas River. This fantastic stretch of land experienced dramatic changes of weather. The weather could, in min-

utes, go from serene and balmy to wild and cold, with hail as big as a man's fist. The wind blew unremittingly, day in and day out, year in and year out, blowing hot and dry in summer, and with a ferocity that permeated the bones in winter. The vast rolling hills, the monotonous landscape unbroken by plow or well, combined with the endless whine of the wind, was enough to drive early settlers and explorers mad. But to the Pawnee it was home.

Here the Pawnee found everything they needed for survival and aesthetic satisfaction. The soil was rich and good for farming. The limitless grasslands extending as far as the eye could see meant food for the buffalo, which roamed the Plains in the millions. The star-laden night sky inspired the Pawnee, who became famous for their astronomical drawings and observations.

For a few hundred years, the Pawnee lived an enviable, golden existence.

Charles Bird King was one of the first non-Indians to paint members of the Pawnee from life. Between 1822 and 1843, King painted 143 different Indian chiefs who visited the president of the United States at the White House. Shown here is his portrait of the Pawnee leader Petalesharro.

PAWNEE
TRIBAL
LIFE

Compared to most of the Plains tribes, the Pawnee's lifestyle was unique. They had two styles of home, the tipi and the earth lodge. The tipi was used for times when the Pawnee were on the hunting trail or warpath, or when they were away from their main camp for long periods of time A tipi could be quickly and single-handedly dismantled, mounted on a travois—a V-shaped frame made with lodge poles, secured to a horse or large dog—and hauled to the next camp site with little trouble. Tipis were constructed with an outer layer of hides, and were surprisingly large, comfortable, and waterproof. Many modern-day tent designs were inspired by the tipi.

The earth lodge was the more permanent dwelling used by the Pawnee. This type of dwelling was usually round, measuring about 40 feet in diameter, with large poles as a frame. The round shape was inspired by the night skies so admired by the Pawnee; they built their homes to mirror the shape of the heavenly dome.

The Pawnee technique of mixing mud, grass, and rocks to fill in the gaps between the poles was imitated by the white settlers who came later and created the now-famous Plains "sod" home.

Each Pawnee village comprised about a dozen earth lodges. Each lodge could comfortably hold as many as eight families, housing a total of around 40 people. The average size village had a population of around 500 Pawnee. The Pawnee lived in their earth lodges for four to six months out of the year. In the spring and fall they lived in these dwellings, planted and harvested their crops, and prepared themselves and their belongings for another migration.

29

Like most other Plains tribes, the Pawnee had rules of etiquette for everyone to follow that helped them to get along. There were quite a number of rules in regard to visiting another lodge or tipi. If the door flap was open, this was a sign that the residents were receptive to visitors. If it was closed, the visitors were to announce their presence and wait to be acknowledged and invited inside.

The warmest place, the place next to the fire, was reserved for visitors. Robes were laid there as a sign of welcome, much the way we place welcome mats at our doors. When entering the lodge or tipi, women followed the men inside. Everyone walked around the entire lodge by way of the east, as there was a sacred spot in every lodge in the west, in front of a buffalo altar. This sacred spot, called *wi-haru*, was reserved for "the place where the wise words of those who have gone before us are resting." It was also considered a breach of etiquette to pass between two people engaged in conversation, or between another person and the fire. Men sat cross-legged. Women sat on their heels or with their legs out to one side.

No one immediately addressed their visitors. There was a pause in which guests were allowed to rest a moment, gather their thoughts, and catch their breath. This was the time for the smoking of the pipe. It was only after the pipe smoking that the business at hand or the reason for the visit was mentioned. If the visitors were unexpected, the nature of their business was not to be asked; the Pawnee were infinitely patient and knew that time would reveal what they needed to know. The order of conversation was determined by one's tribal status.

It was always at the conclusion of any discussion that a woman in the lodge served everyone food; the conversation then turned to lighter matters. If the guests had been expected, they brought their own bowls and eating utensils. It was considered polite to decline nothing and to eat all the food one was served. The end of the evening was marked when the host cleaned his pipe. This was the signal for everyone to leave, and they did so with no further talk.

In addition to the regular lodge, the Pawnee also built a sweat lodge, similar to a steam bath. Cleanliness was highly valued by every member of the tribe and they often bathed not once but twice daily, regardless of the weather. The sweat lodge was used for personal cleansing and purification rituals.

The survival of the people was dependent in large part on the hunting prowess of its men. To provide their families with meat and hides, the mainstays of their existence, hunting was taken extremely seriously and was carried out in a prescribed manner.

Each hunter made his own bows and arrows, and other weapons such as flint knives. The hunting of the buffalo was done in the summer and winter, but although much of their hunting

The Pawnee maintained two types of primary dwelling, the well-known tipi (shown) and the perhaps less familiar earth lodge.

was buffalo related, they also hunted deer, antelope, and elk. The Pawnee hunters were adept at killing jackrabbit and mountain sheep, and they would set snares in which to catch game birds such as quail.

Most of the Pawnee culture centered around the buffalo. For the Pawnee and other Plains tribes, the buffalo was tangible proof that Tirawa cared for them. With the gift of bison, Tirawa provided the people with vir-tually all their needs.

In the spring and fall hunting seasons, the location of the Pawnee campsite was determined by the herd's movements; they traveled where the buffalo did. The holy men helped the people locate the buffalo, as did the various wolf-skin-robed scouts. Medicine bundles often included buffalo parts. The Pawnee burned the Plains grasses each spring to induce new growth upon which the buffalo fed.

The successful hunter made a life study of the buffalo's characteristics and learned them well. He knew there were different colors of buffalo—one might have a spotted coat, another a mouse-colored coat. The older a buffalo was, the tougher his flesh and the rougher his fur would be. Thus, if a bison lived to an old age, he was usually safe from the lance and arrow.

The buffalo were not hunted in July, their mating season. This was a dangerous time for anyone to get near a bull bison, which could be quite aggressive. The young buffalo, called a calf, was born in the spring with a birth weight of up to 40 pounds. The calf's hair was tinged red or yellow; this was replaced by a darker color by the time the calf was a year old. Many Pawnee children wore robes made with the skin of a newborn calf.

By the next fall, the yearling had developed thick, dark, fluffy fur, and his weight had increased to about 400 pounds. A two-year-old calf began to show the beginnings of horns and had two teeth. The most favored hides

The tipi was essentially a mobile home, generally used by the Pawnee when the tribe was on the move, as in following the hunt or relocating because of warfare.

came from four-year-old calves, whose fur was silky and thick.

The Pawnee were very imaginative in using all of the buffalo parts they could; there was very little wasted. Each part had many uses. For example, the skin was tanned for winter robes, headdresses, saddle padding, and ornaments. Horns and bones were used for various types of cooking and cultivating implements and other tools, weapons, and toys. Tendons were dressed and made into especially resilient and strong sinew, which was used for sewing clothing and tipi liners and for making bowstrings. The four-chambered stomach lining was used as a cooking vessel and a type of pail for carrying water. Hooves were used to make ceremonial rattles; dried buffalo dung, or chips, were used to fuel fires. Bison tail hair was braided and made into rope.

Every edible part of the bison was consumed. The tongue and hump were considered delicacies; the liver and heart were often eaten raw, immediately after the kill. Tougher parts of the buffalo were made into pemmican.

The sheer number of buffalo was in itself enough to inspire an almost spiritual awe in the Pawnee. So great were the numbers of buffalo that it would take hours for a single great herd to cross a stream. It was only natural for the Pawnee to base much of their religion upon this great animal. Medicine men used buffalo skulls in performing their ceremonies; a skull was also placed in front of the entrance to the sweat lodge, facing east, the direction of the sunrise.

Every home had a sacred place reminding the inhabitants of the importance of the buffalo to their lives. Each earth lodge had a raised platform, a kind of altar, on the west wall opposite the entryway. This held a buffalo skull; the lodge's sacred medicine bundle and two ears of corn were suspended above it.

The Pawnee supplemented their diet with fish from the surrounding rivers. Fish were caught with a flint-headed spear or a kind of seine made of willow, reeds, or woven strips of hide. Fish of all types were numerous along the big rivers, including a variety of trout, perch, and crappie. Turtles provided a tasty respite from the daily diet.

Pawnee women gathered a great variety of vegetation, taking it as another gift from Tirawa. They foraged for wild peas and over a dozen different types of wild fruit, including persimmons and chokecherries. Prairie turnips (called *pommes blanches* by the French and Indian turnips by white settlers) have been said to be the most widely used wild food source. They ripened in the spring to the size of an egg, and were either eaten raw, cooked in soups, or sliced and sun-dried for later use.

The women also gathered and peeled the sweet thistle plant, which tasted similar to a banana. Milkweed buds, rose hips, and the fruit of the prickly-pear cactus were flavorful and

Earth lodges were the more permanent dwelling places of the Pawnee. Ideally suited for the climate and topography of the Nebraska plains, such earth lodges inspired the sod homes built by so many of the foreign immigrants who settled on the prairie in the 19th century.

nutritious; they were often added to buffalo stews.

Seminomadic as they were, the Pawnee nonetheless stayed long enough in one place to cultivate some crops. They planted corn, squash, pumpkins, melons, and beans. The always practical Pawnee women came up with a clever way to support the bean plants without having to make poles for their gardens. They simply planted the beans at the bases of cornstalks. As the corn grew higher, the beans had a natural pole on which to climb.

Farming was relegated to the Pawnee women. The only Pawnee ceremony in which women played a major role was the one in which the spring crops were planted. This was known as the Ground-Breaking Ceremony. During the wintertime, a woman in the village, specially chosen by Tirawa, would have a vision of the ceremony. She told the priests of the village of her vision. The priests would declare her the "visionary" who would be the sponsor of the Ground-Breaking Ceremony. The visionary's brother or nearest living male relative killed a buffalo especially for her. She dressed it out, prepared the meat, and stored it in a cache, an underground food-storage pit that preserved the meat through the winter.

The tribe's holy men waited for two signs. First, the willows along the river had to bud. Then the moon had to hide herself—what we call the dark of the moon—which the Pawnee saw as the time most favorable for germination. The priests then told the visionary it was time to begin. The visionary arose early the next morning, took a special medicine bundle from its hanging place inside the lodge, and hung it outside on a tripod. She then cleaned the lodge and decorated it with willow sprouts.

The four priests then had the woman bring the meat she had prepared for the ceremony, and they also invited four specially chosen women to participate by donating more dried buffalo meat and corn. The group, with a number of other persons of importance, gathered together in the ceremonial lodge. The visionary did her special dance for the occasion, and the others shook gourd rattles and

sang. Then everyone ate the food that had been brought and stayed up talking and telling stories until the early morning hours.

The next day the Ground-Breaking Ceremony itself took place. The entire ceremony lasted from dawn until sunset. Its major feature was a dance depicting the hoeing of the corn, which was always the first crop to be planted. Then the holy men ritually broke the ground with four sacred hoes. After the Ground-Breaking Ceremony, the actual planting began. The people worked at a fever pitch; it took about six days for the entire garden to be weeded, cultivated, and planted. While planting, the Pawnee women sang special songs to "help" the seeds sprout. One way in which the Pawnee women helped each other was for a group of women to plant and harvest a newly married bride's first crop.

Tobacco was another crop of importance to the Pawnee. The ground for the tobacco field was burned bare of all other vegetation. After the tobacco seeds were planted, the field was carefully weeded. When the crop was ripe, the entire tobacco plant was cut and dried. The part of the tobacco plant with the best flavor for smoking was said to be the unripe seed capsules.

The Plains provided virtually all that the Pawnee people required for food, shelter, clothing, defense, hunting, and artistic expression. Their workshop was the natural world; they took items from the earth, always giving thanks, as these were gifts from Tirawa. They wasted nothing; to do so would have been a sign of ingratitude. Their tools were made of woods, grasses, stones, bones, plants, clays, and the skins and feathers of various animals.

The Pawnee women wove reeds and other natural fibers into mats for their lodge floors and bedding materials. Natural fiber wraps were also used to encase the deceased. These natural fibers were also woven into carrying baskets and small gaming implements, such as gambling trays. A stiff type of grass, called porcupine grass, was made into a kind of hairbrush.

Wood was often made into bowls and mortars, pipe stems, and ceremonial objects. Spoons with beaded handles were made from wood as well as stone. Wood from the elm, chokecherry, dogwood, birch, and willow (among others) went into the making of arrow shafts and bows. Because it was strong yet light, cottonwood was used in tipi and earth lodge construction. The Pawnee were more adept at carpentry than many other Plains tribes. They showed their talents particularly in the making of post-and-beam fittings for their earth lodge frames.

In the making of bull (or basket) boats, the people were once again practical and ingenious in adapting to their environment. The shallow Platte River was virtually unnavigable by the average vessel. But the Pawnee's bull boat was light, with little draft, and

was the vessel of choice when the Pawnee plied the waters of the wide Platte.

Stones were sculpted for use as pipe bowls, spoons, and other hollowware for eating and cooking. Buffalo horns were polished, hollowed, and used as quivers for holding arrows. At first, flint and other types of hard stones and bones were made into arrowheads; later, trade with other peoples made possible metal arrowheads.

There were basically two types of arrowhead—one used in hunting and one used for war. The hunting arrowhead was long, barbless, and tapering. It was firmly attached to the shaft of the arrow. In this way, after the kill, the entire weapon could be easily removed, saving it for another hunt.

The war arrowhead was made to function in just the opposite manner. It was heavier than a hunting arrowhead, and its head was barbed to make extraction nearly impossible (not to mention excruciating for the wounded warrior). The war arrowhead was attached to the shaft in such a way that, with any effort made to remove it from a wound, the shaft and head would separate. If this happened the wounded warrior would almost certainly suffer a painful and drawn-out death.

Arrow shafts were painted to identify their owner. This was particularly useful in a large hunting group, such as accompanied the semiannual buffalo hunt; everyone knew in this way

These Pawnee warriors were photographed beside an earth lodge in Nebraska in 1871. Their dress is a combination of items of traditional Pawnee garb, such as buffalo robes and bear claw necklaces, and outside manufacture, such as peace medals and government blankets.

which animals were their responsibility to butcher.

In processing killed animals, stones and bones played extremely useful roles. Both were used in the cutting of flesh, in the making of tools from various animal parts, and in the sewing of animal hides to make clothes and tipi covers. Sharp, broad stones were also used in food preparation, especially in the making of pemmican, a nutritious blend of pulverized berries mixed with buffalo meat and tallow. Many larger bones were used

in agriculture. The broad, strong shoulder blade of the buffalo, for example, was used as a spade or a hoe.

Most of the plants important to the Pawnee were of the edible variety. But besides weaving grasses for mats, the Pawnee used various plants in the dyeing and decorating of their clothes, tipis, or possessions, such as a pipe stem or a war pony's hide. Many hide blankets were dyed black with water boiled with sumac leaves.

The pigments in various types of earth were used in painting, as well as

A rare photograph of the inside of a Pawnee earth lodge. Such dwellings might house as many as eight families.

in the dyeing of hides. To dye a hide blanket white, for example, a fine white clay was rubbed into the hide after tanning, then allowed to dry before being removed.

Clay was used primarily in the making of pottery, a talent for which the Pawnee are especially noted. The making of clay into pottery required many steps. First, a mold was made from a smoothed-out tree trunk. Then stones were "roasted" for a long time in a hot fire, ground, and made into a fine powder. This powder was mixed with clay, then smeared over the mold which was well greased with buffalo fat. While the clay was still pliable, the Pawnee made sharp marks in the sides for ornamentation, then lifted it from the mold. The clay form was then burned in the fire. While it was baking, the Pawnee put corn in the pot and stirred it, making a kind of natural glaze on the inside of the pot.

The resulting pottery was extremely hard and durable enough to hang over a cooking fire. Pottery excavated from Pawnee villages has a shape characteristic of the Pawnee method of pottery making, with a large, globular bottom and a thick rim. This rim was used by the cook, who secured a rawhide "handle" around it, to carry it or hang it from the cooking fire.

The skins of animals were also important to Pawnee daily life and survival. Tipi covers, moccasins, saddles, ropes and whips, parfleches, and a kind of a water bucket all came from various types of hide. Hides also went into the making of skin shirts, which were worn by men of high standing.

There were basically three stages of skin, or hide, preparation. The first stage produced rawhide, in which the hair was removed from the skin. The second stage—tanning—produced a hide that was softer and more pliable than rawhide. To tan, the hide was stretched on a kind of frame, and a mixture of elm bark and buffalo brains was worked into the hide. Skins could be tanned with or without hair.

The third step in hide preparation was dyeing. Hides were often dyed a light yellow color by smoking them over a fire made with rotten wood. Clothing was usually dyed this color; the skins most often used for clothing were deer and elk, as they were the softest.

Feathers were used on headdresses, fans, lances, war clubs, coup sticks, shields, hair decorations, and pipe stems. In feathering, or fletching, arrow shafts, the feathers were placed in such a way as to give a spin to the loosed arrow, giving it a motion similar to that of a bullet fired from a rifled gun. This made the trajectory of the arrow more stable and accurate. Feathers were usually obtained from the eagle, wild turkey, hawk, and owl.

Preparation for the actual hunt was a protracted process involving travel, ceremony, and discipline. Once the traveling band got near a herd, the entire camp of men, women, and children were under a certain amount of restraint. This restraint was ensured by a special society, the Hunt Police. The night before the big hunt, a group of men were appointed for this job. The police would then patrol the camp to make certain that all was quiet and that no hunter had gone out alone. If this happened, even though he might get one buffalo, the entire herd could be stampeded and the tribe could lose its chance at getting enough meat for everyone.

The dog that barked unnecessarily that night might be killed on the spot. Children were not allowed to cry or play any noisy games. The people were not even allowed to chop wood.

Hours before dawn, several scouts were assigned to a reconnaissance mission. Getting very close to the herd, the scouts would crawl on their bellies, imitating the wolf, of which the bison were not afraid. Sometimes the scouts would even wear wolf skins.

Returning to the camp, the scouts

would tell of the number and location of the herd; the chiefs would devise a plan from this information. The women broke camp quickly, taking care to free up as many horses as possible for the hunt. As the people continued these preparations, the medicine man, or shaman, would dance in the impersonation of a buffalo and sing a chant that went something like this:

Now you are going to trot
Buffalo who are killed falling.

He would then fall down as if dead for anyone in the camp who would give him tobacco.

One of the chiefs made a member of the hunting party the official starter, or "hand waver." As they rode closer to the herd, one of the scouts would signal how fast to come and in what direction, depending on what he thought the buffalo herd was about to do. Sometimes the hand waver would hesitate, inadvertently testing the hunters' patience. He waited until he felt his own personal medicine was as good as it was going to get. Any hunter starting before the signal would often get a severe clubbing by the Hunt Police; order was, therefore, usually not difficult to maintain.

At the signal, the hunters sped toward the herd, sometimes shouting to each other the equivalent of "That one's going to be mine!" Any good Pawnee hunter could fire arrows almost as fast as a rifleman could shoot, and they sometimes did it with such force that an arrow would go completely through the animal.

The Pawnee custom was to have two main meals each day. Although most of the food preparation was done by women, the chores were divided so that no one did more than their fair share. In the earth lodge, the women on the south side prepared one meal, the women on the north the other. Each side fed all the occupants of the earth lodge, or about fifty persons. Willing hands were never lacking, as it was an honor to volunteer to work in any capacity that would benefit everyone. Laziness or the shirking of one's duties was unheard of.

The mainstay of each meal was first buffalo and then corn. Corn was prepared in many ways. It was boiled, dried, roasted, made into a mush, added to soup or stew, or pounded to a powder and used as flour. The pottery mentioned earlier was the type of cooking vessel most commonly used by the Pawnee, although there are some accounts of their making stews and soups using the stomach lining from a buffalo. Since this type of cooking vessel was not fireproof, however, the stew was cooked by dropping in large stones that were first heated in a fire. The hot stones were stirred around in the food mixture, cooking the stew quickly.

Drying foodstuffs, especially meats, was an ingenious method of food preservation devised by the Pawnee and other food-gathering peoples. Pawnee women stored preserved

Pawnee women fashion the framework for an earth lodge. With Pawnee men responsible for hunting, the women of the tribe took care of the home and raised crops.

food in a pit dug out of the ground. Called a cache, this pit kept foods cool and dry and delayed the process of decay. The pit was usually about 11 feet deep and bell-shaped, with smooth walls. The floor was covered with sand and then bark. Explorers such as Lewis and Clark were quick to take note of this ingenious method of food storage and preservation; they employed it in their travels, digging caches in places to which they intended to return.

When a woman cooked a meal, she did virtually every step in its preparation herself. The vegetables and fruits had been raised and gathered by her own hands. She had butchered and dried the meat she served; the bread came from a grain that she herself grew and made into flour. She had most likely dug the cache and made the cooking implements, such as the pottery, the wooden bowls and spoons, and even the grass mats upon which everyone sat.

Women's everyday clothing consisted of a buckskin dress or wraparound skirt with an overblouse and leggings. If the weather was fair, children of both sexes often wore nothing when they were very young. Later, a girl's clothing was a smaller version of what her mother wore. For special occasions, the leggings were beaded and painted.

Men's and boys' clothing usually consisted of a breechclout (a type of loincloth), a buckskin shirt, and leggings. The shirt was usually worn loose. The Pawnee man wore not one but two belts. The first belt held up his breechclout and leggings. The second was made from thick hide and on this belt he hung his tomahawk, knife, and gun, as well as his pipe, tobacco pouch, and whetstone.

Every man had a buffalo robe that he kept close at hand in his lodge. He threw it over his shoulders or around his waist to receive visitors. Those in high standing wore special clothing. The skin shirt was for those in the very highest of ranks and regard. This shirt was decorated with scalps lining the sleeves, and porcupine quillwork running the length of the shirt front. A man who had done exceptionally well in battle wore an otter skin around his neck. Many warriors wore turbans of different colors and designs to denote their rank.

Moccasins were left plain for everyday use but were decorated for special occasions. Burial moccasins were usually beaded and painted. Festival moccasins and wedding moccasins were beaded and decorated with elaborate quillwork. The Pawnee, like many other tribes of the Plains, had their own uniquely shaped and decorated style of moccasin. Following the trail of the enemy was thus made easier; however, sometimes a warrior would steal moccasins from a fallen enemy and wear those to throw off any would-be pursuers.

So closely did the Pawnee people relate to the heavenly beings that they considered their earth lodges to be smaller versions of the universe. The lodge was built in such a way that, through the smoke hole at the top, the western stars could be observed, and the eastern skies could be viewed through the door flap. Just before dawn and right after sunset, the people would observe the horizon, taking note of the position and courses of the stars.

The performance of rituals and chores, such as the Morning Star Ceremony and the planting of the garden, centered around these cosmic observations. When on the hunt, the way in which the Pawnee grouped their tipis followed an astronomical pattern, mimicking what they saw in the sky. The Pawnee had an acute sense of the position and order of the stars, and they are noted for their artistic interpretations of the heavens. For

A gathering of Pawnee men prepares to slice a watermelon. Though seminomadic, the Pawnee nevertheless cultivated a large variety of crops.

example, rawhide containers in which they packed dried buffalo meat were painted with cosmic designs. Different patterns and colors were used for the moon, stars, and even the time of night. The artist who painted these designs had to be specially trained and had to possess the proper religious qualifications.

One type of Pawnee warbonnet was fashioned after a comet. The bonnet was decorated with eagle feathers, long strings of white beads (symbolizing the comet's "tail") and a large shiny disk made with a black oyster shell.

Knowledge of the constellations also had a more practical use. A person could easily become disoriented on the vast Plains, much in the same way that a sailor at sea, without knowledge of the stars, might lose his way. The earliest explorers were amazed at how adept the Pawnee were in traveling across the Plains and at how they always knew their precise location.

The chief of the tribe held his power through divine ordinance

A Pawnee man wraps himself in a buffalo robe as he faces the camera. Such robes were worn with the fur side in; the skin side was often decorated, as with the star design shown here.

chief. The chief was no great wielder of power. His position was more like the head of a very large family, a sort of administrative official. This was a natural outcome of the Pawnee way of voluntarism and independence, and it suited their lifestyle well.

There were occasions when the son of a chief also attained chiefdom, but a spirit of humility, calm wisdom, and cooperation played a more important role in the people's choice. When a chief took note of a promising young man with ambitions to become a chief, the older man would take the younger man into his lodge to serve a kind of apprenticeship.

The Pawnee community also had shamans, or medicine men. The term "medicine man" is a word first employed by European explorers, who witnessed shamanistic activities without understanding them. In Pawnee culture there existed what have been called "doctor cults." These were organizations of men who practiced varying kinds and degrees of medicine and were more akin to clubs than cults.

The Pawnee believed there were two separate realms, one of the sky and one of the earth and water. The holy man was consulted about all things having to do with the sky, such as cosmic ceremonies. These included the Morning Star, harvesting, planting, and creation ceremonies. The shaman was concerned with the animals, including humankind, who were part of the earth and water.

The shamans believed that long

because his wisdom was a gift from Tirawa. He was also in possession of the tribe's sacred bundle, given to them by First Man. However, there was no one chief over all four Pawnee bands; rather, each village had its own ago Tirawa had entered a man's dreams, teaching him the wisdom of the animals. The man learned about the healing power of special herbs, roots, and songs. That is how shamanism came to the people. When someone, in a dream or vision, received a sign that he too should become a shaman, he would apprentice himself to one. As an apprentice, he sometimes shared the lodge, ran errands, and cooked and served meals when the shamans were in council.

After his apprenticeship, the new shaman was elected into one of eight "doctor cults." Each cult held at least two ceremonies a year, as well as "mesmerizing contests," as any good shaman was also skilled in hypnotism. The cults occasionally gathered together into one large-scale "Doctor Lodge." If a person was found to be conducting medical or ceremonial practices and was not a member of a cult, that person was considered a witch and treated with contempt.

Although it appears that the Pawnee lodge was matriarchal in nature, many of the tasks of men and women were shared. Men as well as women were able cooks and adept at tasks such as sewing and child care. Pawnee women were generally held in high esteem. In preparing and providing food, clothing, and shelter for her family, in the bearing and rearing of children, and in her duties of moving the camp, the Pawnee woman did her chores with dignity and a sense of pride and fulfillment.

With the rough life into which children were born, infant mortality was relatively high. Children were therefore highly regarded. Children ensured continuity for the people; they were possessors of the future. Boys had more of a social life than girls. In general, children were allowed to play only with those children whose parents held similar rank.

Men could make themselves near-legendary figures in the eyes of the people by their valor in battle or on the hunt. Warriors most often brought honor to themselves by "counting coup," touching an enemy without killing him, which took unusual courage if he were armed. Warriors carried "coup sticks" expressly for this purpose. To a lesser degree, the taking of scalps was also considered a form of counting coup, as was the stealing of horses.

Hunters were important to the tribe because they provided the people with food. Hunters usually dressed plainly, unless they were engaged in what has been termed a "formal" buffalo hunt. This hunt usually included more than one band; there might be up to a hundred men participating. For the formal buffalo hunt, the men dressed in specially decorated leggings and moccasins; those of exceptional rank or prowess wore a skin shirt or tied a bright red bandanna around their heads. The hunting horses were painted in the same manner as their masters. Hunt Police carried clubs and wore belts to symbolize their office.

Warriors and hunters took part in ceremonies and rituals before a battle, raid, or hunt. Warriors also played a major role in harvesttime ceremonies. The dress of warriors in actual battle was as little as the weather would permit, usually little more than moccasins and a breechclout. The ever practical Pawnee understood that clothing entering the skin along with a bullet or arrow was what caused the most pain and subsequent infection.

As with other aspects of Pawnee life, the activity of going to battle was accompanied by song. One song warriors sang as they rode along goes like this:

Let us see, is this real,
This life I am living?
Ye Gods who dwell everywhere,
Let us see, is this real,
This life I am living?

Perhaps the song expressed a fear of dying and the transitory nature of life. Even strong warriors sought to make sense of the constant struggle to survive, long before the name of any god other than Tirawa was spoken in their realm.

Pawnee society also featured a number of specialized societies, clubs, or clans. Hunters, warriors, or even women of vision could be in specialized societies, which held ceremonies and dances when the stars were auspicious. The cults, or clubs, had such names as Black-tailed Deer, Eagle, Reindeer, Buffalo, and Coyote. One such club, the Society of Lucky Children, was not comprised of children but adults. In their gatherings, they sat on their mats and recounted lucky things that had happened to them, their tribe, or their ancestors.

The Pawnee language derives from its Caddoan ancestry and is a language group shared by the Caddo, Wichita, Arikara, and Pawnee peoples. Of the Pawnee's four bands, however, the Skidi or "Wolf" band speaks a different dialect from the other three, probably because it is more separate geographically.

The linguistic diversity between tribes created a need for intertribal communication. Some say that it was a need for trade between tribes that led to the development of sign language; but regardless, this intertribal language of the Plains nations is a beautiful and graceful thing to behold. Sign language was practical in that communication could be accomplished even if the communicants were a certain distance apart, which helped if they were uncertain if they were speaking to friend or foe. Some experts have pointed to a relationship between sign language and Native American pictographs. Many single signs spoke entire phrases or sentences. The "speaker" could also communicate with movements of his horse.

Other ways of signaling over long distances included the use of ropes, blankets, mirrors, or smoke signals. At close range, such as in battle, flags, lances, or hand and arm signals would

This Pawnee man is wearing one of the various peace medals issued to the tribe at different times by the U.S. government. He is wrapped in a traditional buffalo robe and brandishes a pistol obtained in trade with whites.

be employed. Whistles made from the bone of a turkey leg or an eagle's wing were used in such a way as to be heard over the din of battle. With a series of prearranged whistles, the warring party would know whether they should attack or retreat.

One practice unique to the Pawnee that they clung to even into the 19th century was that of human sacrifice. The Morning Star Ceremony was the second spring ritual conducted by the tribal holy men, the first being the retelling of the creation myth. The Morning Star Ceremony included the sacrifice of a young girl taken from an enemy tribe. The Pawnee believed that this sacrifice was to repay the Morning Star god for his efforts during the earth's creation, and to ensure a good crop and fertility among their women. Since they also believed that the first person on earth had been female, in this way they symbolically "returned" her to Morning Star.

The ceremony began with a young warrior having a vision of the Morning Star speaking to him. The warrior told a tribal priest. They then shared a ceremonial pipe. The warrior chose a small contingent to go with him to abduct the maiden to be sacrificed. The priest ceremonially prepared and dressed the warrior in a buffalo-hair rope belt, a collar made of otter skin, a hawk's skin around his neck, and an ear of corn on his left shoulder. His face was painted with two streaks of red down each cheek and a bird's footprint on his forehead.

Dressed in this way, the warrior and his companions departed as the Morning Star once again rose. Approaching the enemy camp (some accounts say it was usually a Sioux tribe), the Pawnee band surrounded them and attacked on a given signal. They were instructed to harm no one unless it was necessary, but to look for a girl of thirteen who would then be pronounced holy for the Great Star.

The group carried the girl back to camp, where she was well treated until the holy men deemed it was the right time for the ceremony. The girl was then given a smoke bath, which was done by having her pass over a fire made with sweet-smelling grasses. This was done to further purify her. She was painted with a mixture of red pigment and buffalo fat and dressed in fine calfskin, a thick buffalo robe, and soft down moccasins. The girl was also given special eating utensils, to be used only by her.

For several days the unsuspecting maiden was treated with utmost respect and feted with singing and dancing and feasting, even as the sacrificial scaffold was being prepared. Finally, as dawn approached on the appointed day, the procession to the scaffold began. All male members of the tribe were to take part. The visionary warrior, dressed in his ceremonial clothing, tied the girl's wrists with elk-skin rope and led the procession. Four holy men carried sacred bundles, each representing one of the cardinal directions. On the way to the scaffold, the

(Continued on page 57)

PAINTING THE PAST

Born and raised in Pawnee, Oklahoma, in 1944, artist Charles W. Chapman made his living riding bulls, building houses, and raising race horses for many years. In his spare time, he taught himself to paint, eventually working exclusively in oil. In 1986, Chapman was awarded a Special Merit Award at the Tahlequah Trail of Tears Art Show and decided to become a full-time artist. His works have won numerous prizes, including first place at the 1988 and 1989 Tulsa Arts Festival and best of show at the 1988 Cimarron Western Arts Show. In 1989 the White House honored Chapman by holding an exhibition of his paintings.

Chapman's paintings celebrate his Pawnee heritage. He extensively researches Pawnee history and tradition for his works, which are notable not only for their artistic merit but also for their historical accuracy.

A number of Chapman's canvases depict actual Pawnee shamans from the past as they looked while staging their ceremonies. Chapman continues to live in Pawnee, where he paints and raises horses.

Skiri Scout (1988)

49

The General (1995)

The Victor (1994)

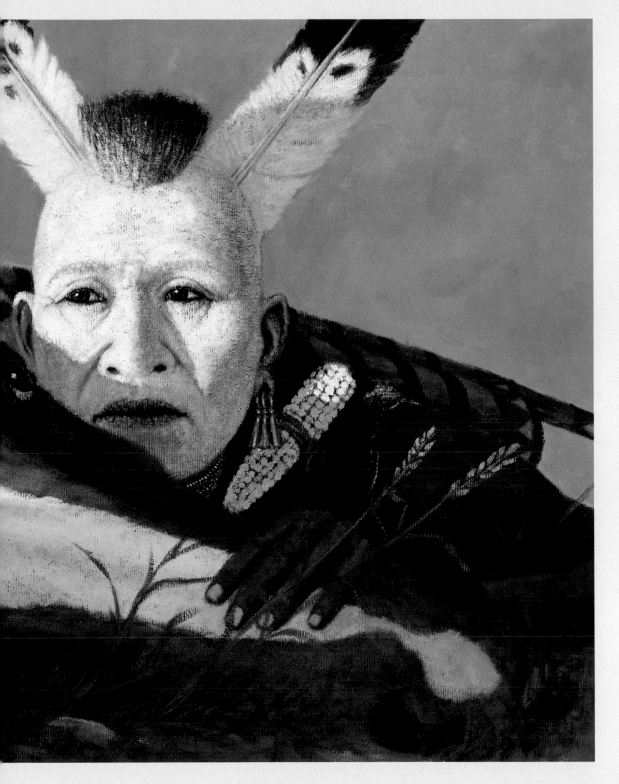

War Collar (1995)

54

Good Buffalo (1989)

Wolf Signals (1993)

(Continued from page 48)

people sang four songs for the animals the Evening Star had placed in the semicardinal directions—the bear, the mountain lion, the wildcat, and the wolf.

The girl was led atop the scaffold and bound by her wrists, standing upright, facing the direction of the sunrise. Without warning, just as the sun rose, one of the holy men ran up to the maiden and shot her through the heart with his bow and arrow. Some of her blood was used to anoint a specially consecrated buffalo heart and tongue, which were then ceremonially burned. Afterward, each male of the tribe, even the little babies, who of course needed help, shot an arrow into the maiden's body. After this, she was taken down and returned to earth to allow her blood to fertilize the ground. The Morning Star Ceremony was followed by much celebration and what one witness described as "ceremonial sexual licensure."

The ages considered most auspicious for marriage were 15 for girls and 18 for boys, but with first marriages for both sexes there was often as much as a 15-year age difference between husband and wife. The reason for this was that a mature man was expected to care not only for his new wife but for her entire family as well. After marriage, the husband usually lived with his wife's family; the family thus looked upon suitors in terms of their ability to become providers for the family group.

Young boys were often married to older women who were not in as much need of a provider as were their younger counterparts. When they matured into grown men, they would then choose a younger bride. In this way, the needs of the mature and the needs of the young who were unable to provide for themselves were all met. Though the idea of polygamy may be offensive to our modern sensibility, it worked out well for the Pawnee at the height of their civilization.

A woman's hand was sought with the giving of gifts. If she were quite young and unmarried, her suitor might bring as many as half a dozen horses to her father's herd. The bride-price of a mature woman might be one or two horses; these were given to her nearest male relative, such as a brother.

With such fluid relationships, the Pawnee were not without some rules. The paternity of children had to be absolutely certain. Toward this end, a woman was "faithful" to one man for one month at a time. When she discovered her pregnancy, she would thus be able to point out his obligations to the soon-to-be-father. The father was expected to provide for his offspring, regardless of whose lodge they resided in. If any woman broke this rule of "serial monogamy," it would be the resulting offspring who would suffer. Children without clear paternity were regarded as outcasts by the entire tribe.

A lodge's occupants changed each time the people returned from the buffalo hunt. A family that had been in one lodge for a season might desire to

Photographed by William Henry Jackson in 1871, Petalesharro holds a peace pipe, which Pawnee men would smoke communally on ceremonial and social occasions.

lodge with a different group the next season. This allowed the Pawnee to cultivate an even greater spirit of inter-dependence and cooperation.

Families lived in ways that would teach the young a spirit of cooperation and provide both young and old with constant companionship and a sense of security. The idea of a nursing home, for example, is completely alien to traditional Pawnee philosophy.

Certain aspects of Pawnee home life seem to have been matriarchal in nature. As mentioned earlier, the food-preparation chores of the earth lodge were equally divided by women in the north and south sectors of the lodge. Other chores were divided mostly according to age. Places the women assumed within the lodge itself were also determined by age.

The mature women occupied the central portion of the lodge's north and south sectors; their chores were to provide the main provisions and direct the efforts of the other women. In the western sectors of these two halves, the young girls and newlywed women resided; the eastern sectors were taken by the elderly women. They were placed here because, symbolically, they were on their way out of life, and were thus placed near the door.

The able hunter was the nucleus of each lodge, but men in general could sleep anywhere they chose. Young men might stay in any lodge on any given night; for them, sleeping mats were placed between the central pillars of the lodge. Old men were also free to stay wherever they pleased, usually becoming an overnight guest of the lodge in which they fell asleep telling stories to the occupants.

The married man's household, that of his wife, was not considered his real home. He lived in his wife's lodge because of his obligations to their marriage and to her family. Sometimes his duties might overwhelm him; then he would leave for a few days and stay at the home of his sisters or mother. This was always considered his real home, and the wife was expected to understand.

There were other men who never had any real responsibilities within the tribe. These men the people called boys regardless of their age. The boys roamed about freely and gave away their possessions even as they obtained them. Sometimes they were recognized as braves for their service to the people.

During pregnancy, many women of the Plains tribes practiced walking in the early morning hours because they believed that this was the time of day the baby grew. Before the baby's birth, the mother or grandmother would make special "medicine" for the child, in the form of two beaded and quilled amulets. One was in the form of a lizard, which they believed frightened away malevolent forces; the other was a turtle, known for its longevity and for being difficult to kill. These amulets would be particularly useful if the infant were a boy.

When it came time for the child to be born, a woman in labor usually went to her home lodge. If the tribe were on the move, she had to give birth out in the open alongside the trail.

Older women attended the birth. The physician or shaman might also attend, singing songs to ensure an easy delivery and a healthy infant. If things got difficult, the priest would come and decorate the turtle amulet with a tortoise charm, to shield the baby from any dangers in the birthing process.

After birth, the umbilical cord was severed, wrapped in herbs or tobacco, and packed inside the turtle amulet. This amulet was later worn on the child's clothing as a reminder of the gift of life it had received from its parents. If a warrior attained greatness, he might wear this amulet on his headdress. Several days after birth, the baby was given a name, usually by the father. This name might be changed later if the child, especially a boy child, achieved high status within the tribe or had a life-changing experience.

When an elderly Pawnee felt that he or she had had enough of life, that person would simply walk away from the village and never return. But when people fell ill and died, or were killed in battle or in the hunt, they were given a burial whenever possible. The deceased were dressed in their best clothes, and specially beaded burial moccasins were placed on their feet. The deceased was often wrapped in a blanket or a covering made of reeds, grasses, or hide. The body was laid to rest in a high place, to be nearer the Creator, usually in a burial scaffold or tree. The family would also hang some of the deceased's favorite possessions nearby. If the dead person had been a great warrior, his favorite horse would sometimes be killed to accompany him to the other side, although this might be protested by family members hoping to inherit the animal. A grieving widow often cut off her hair and at least one of her fingers.

Among Native American peoples, grave robbing was unheard of; places of burial were considered inviolable. Even if a weaponless, hungry warrior, lost from his tribe, came upon a burial site in which there were plenty of knives, guns, and other provisions, he would not desecrate the site by stealing.

Babies and children in Pawnee society were considered gifts from Tirawa and thus were treated with a great deal of indulgence that was sometimes frowned upon by early white explorers. Since their lives were centered in a group of intermingled personalities from their earliest days, Pawnee children learned from and were cared for by a myriad of persons in the tribe.

Formal discipline was not really needed by Pawnee children. The greatest disciplinarian was the children's environment. Pawnee children were taught from their first breath that strict self-control and cooperation were intrinsic to their survival. Every day they were shown harsh examples of what would happen if they were to do otherwise.

A hunter going out alone, in defiance of the Hunt Police, might be ambushed and killed by a marauding enemy band. He might stampede the buffalo herd upon which the tribe depended, which could result in a food shortage. Children learned by example to be honorable, courageous, industrious, and generous, and grew to dread anything that would bring them the contempt or criticism of their peers.

Right after a child was weaned, he or she was given over to the "grandmother," who was often an unrelated elderly woman. She was then the major provider for the child's care. The child shared the same bed and even the same meal bowl with the grandmother.

At play, children mimicked their elders. Girls played with miniature tipis and tiny dolls in cradle-boards made with sticks. Boys played games in which they pretended to "count coup," or kill buffalo. But when boys and girls reached the age of adolescence, they were no longer allowed to play together.

When a Pawnee boy reached the age of about ten, the mother often sent him to her brother's lodge. The uncle then taught the boy all he would need to know for survival and life. This instruction went as far as the sharing of the uncle's wife (or wives) with the nephew. When the boy was about 12, he went on his first hunt with his fellow tribesmen. Later, he would accompany his father and perhaps an uncle or two on a raid of an enemy camp. The Pawnee knew that praise early on was an invaluable teaching tool and gave it as often as possible.

Girls were taught at an early age to think of their future responsibilities.

A Pawnee mother, father, and child. The Pawnee regarded the proper raising of children as the responsibility of the entire tribe, not just the parents.

This photograph of a group of Pawnee men, taken in the early 20th century, demonstrates a variety of traditional clothing styles.

They were encouraged to have their own beds as early as possible, and not to be coddled. Girls were raised to expect that one day they would care for their brothers much as their mother did. Even once established in lodges of their own, their home was always considered their brothers' "real" home, regardless of who each married. The fathers would sometimes tell the sons,

"Be nice to your sister; one day she'll be taking care of you."

As the girl grew into womanhood, she learned and became proficient in all the important things a Pawnee woman needed to know. She learned to sew moccasins, fashion beadwork, cook, and dress and tan buffalo hides and other game. By the time she was of marriageable age, she could dismantle a tipi, load a travois, and be on the move in less than half an hour. She was advised by the older women how to receive suitors and care for the family she would one day have. The Pawnee female was raised to take pride in herself as a woman and in all her accomplishments. A woman who was thrifty, talented, and industrious earned the respect and admiration of all the people.

Pawnee society as a whole was rather fluid, with no firmly established mores, values, or punishments forcibly imposed on the people. When some-one committed a socially repugnant act, he or she was treated as a social outcast. Outcasts were typically children with no clear paternity or people accused of witchcraft. But there was another type of outcast: the person who had been scalped, who could never return to the tribe. They lived on the fringes of the populace and were regarded with fear. The scalped person, even though he or she had survived such an ordeal, was forced to live alone, in a dugout in an embankment, stealing whatever they needed to survive.

The first significant contact between the Pawnee and the whites occurred when Spanish forces under the leadership of Francisco Vasquez de Coronado invaded the American Southwest in 1539.

THE
PAWNEE
WORLD
CHANGES
FOREVER

For centuries, the Pawnee lived a challenging but golden existence in relative peace. Then the season of change was upon them.

The first non–Native American people to meet the Pawnee were the members of a Spanish expedition headed by Francisco Vásquez de Coronado. It was the middle of the 16th century and the world was witnessing international upheaval. Henry VIII of England declared himself king of Ireland, and married and then beheaded his fifth wife, Catherine Howard. In Japan, Portuguese explorers landed, bringing firearms to Asia. The Vatican intensified its campaign to root out heresy through the Inquisition. Many countries were seeking to expand their landholdings, including Spain.

The 29-year-old Coronado was dispatched to "New Spain," as the American territories were called, with 300 Spanish conquistadors, 800 Indian allies, five Franciscan priests, and a few black slaves. Coronado's ambition was to explore New Spain's northernmost boundaries and to move beyond them into the wilderness. The Spanish crown believed that located in this area were several cities of such wealth that they were made of gold. Coronado himself believed this to the extent that he provided nearly half the funds for the expedition—roughly $2 million in today's currency.

Coronado and his men traveled across Texas, Oklahoma, and on into the territory of Kansas. A slave had assured them that there was indeed a golden city there, called Quivira. Once in this region, Coronado and his men were rewarded not with gold but with winds gusting up to 80 miles an hour, shadeless plains with wildly erratic weather, and huge herds of buffalo resembling great dark clouds as they thundered across the Plains. This was about as far north as Coronado would travel in his search for the fabled Seven Cities of Gold. He had been on the trail of Quivira for over a year by the time his soldiers first saw the Pawnee.

A reconnaissance group sent farther north came upon a large Pawnee tribe encamped on the present-day Republican River. The Pawnee were probably astonished to see men wearing metal armor and helmets, with hairy faces (Pawnee men plucked all their facial hair), sitting astride great four-footed beasts that did the work of camp dogs but were large enough to be ridden.

The Pawnee were quick to obtain these wonderful new animals for themselves, using various means to do so. The Pawnee and other Plains tribes came to know that wherever explorers, hunters, and trappers were, horses would be found. They went on increasingly daring raids for horses and whatever other plunder they could take.

The coming of the horse to Pawnee life and culture enlarged their hunting area, made traveling easier and faster, and helped make warriors more effective in battle. The horse also made the Pawnee women's work easier. Instead of loading a travois onto the back of a working dog, a woman could now load not only tipi implements but other things that she might otherwise have carried herself. Children, who

before had to be carried, rode on horseback or atop a travois. The number of horses one owned became a status symbol; the giving of horses in settling a dispute or as a bride-price became part of Pawnee culture.

Between Coronado's explorations in 1541 and the beginning of the 19th century, the Pawnee people enjoyed a time of prosperity and power. Then their land was sold in a deal struck between Napoléon Bonaparte of France and President Thomas Jefferson of the United States. Under the reign of King Louis XVI, France had acquired land in the New World from Spain. In 1803, the new ruler of France, Napoléon, needed money to finance an anticipated war with England. He agreed to sell the land to the Americans. In what has since been called "the greatest diplomatic coup in American history," the United States was able to double its size through this one real estate transaction. For a mere $15 million, the country had obtained had an additional 830,000 square miles of territory.

With the Louisiana Purchase, the U.S. acquired lands extending from the Mississippi River west to the Rockies, from Texas and Louisiana north to the Canadian border. But America would have to impose her sovereignty upon the newly acquired territory. Opposition to this came not only from Native Americans but from Great Britain, Russia, and Spain. Spain in fact refused to recognize the validity of the deal and threatened military expeditions to enforce its claim that the borders of New Spain extended north to the Platte River.

Claims to new territories were easier to enforce if those territories were settled, and to settle them it was first necessary to explore and map them. Meriwether Lewis, then a secretary to the president, and William Clark, were appointed to lead an expedition into the newly acquired wilderness. The discoveries of the Lewis and Clark Expedition made them perhaps the most celebrated of American explorers, and helped to establish the idea that it was America's Manifest Destiny to extend her boundaries all the way to the Pacific Ocean.

In 1806, another adventurer and explorer, Zebulon Pike, was charged with advising all the Native Americans he encountered that their first loyalties were to the United States and not to Spain, and reminding English traders that they were doing business on American soil. But Spain sent Don Facundo Malgares with an army of 600 dragoons who impressed the Pawnee, among others. Seeing his force of men and mounted militia, the Pawnee readily accepted Spanish flags and medals, swore allegiance to Spain, and promised to turn back any American explorers or settlers coming into the disputed lands.

Within days after Malgares's visit, Zebulon Pike encountered the Pawnee. He had only a small band of 19 men and was not in a position to impress the tribe with American might. The Pawnee chief, Sharitarish,

Colonel Zebulon Pike of the U.S. Army made contact with the Pawnee in 1807 when his expedition of exploration blundered into Spanish lands.

told Pike to turn back. If he did not turn back on his own, Chief Sharitarish threatened, his people would turn him back themselves. Pike brazenly refused to back down. Disconcerted by this unexpected show of foolish bravery, they let him pass.

Pike and his men followed the trail of Malgares. Losing him, they then stumbled into Spanish territory and were made prisoners of war. For four months, Zebulon Pike was held in Chihuahua; upon his release in 1807, he gave the American government a detailed account of Spanish military positions, commanders, and other useful strategic information.

Other visitors to Pawnee territory were thirsty not for gold or the thrill of discovery but for the glory of God. Missionaries, sometimes called Black Robes, invaded the lands of the Pawnee on an errand of a spiritual nature. While the Pawnee people had Tirawa and other lesser gods, the missionaries brought them a new, all-powerful God, one of fire and brimstone.

The missionaries not only taught a faith; they changed the lives of countless Native Americans forever. Before they could accept and internalize the teachings of this new God, the Pawnee had to betray their ancestry and culture and become like white people. One Pawnee in particular whose life was affected by the new explorers and their beliefs was Knife Chief. In 1817 he met with William Clark, who had been named superintendent of Indian affairs and was residing in St. Louis. Clark impressed upon Knife Chief the great numbers of white people who would be coming, white people whose beliefs were very different from those of the Pawnee. Knife Chief and his son, Man Chief (or Petalesharro, as he is sometimes called), became increasingly troubled by the sacrificial rites of the Morning Star Ceremony. Finally, Man Chief took action to end the practice. On the dawn of the Morning Star Ceremony in 1817, he rode through a crowd of over 400 warriors and cut the

elk-skin-bound Sioux maiden, Haxti, from the scaffold at the critical moment. Because of Petalesharro's efforts, human sacrifice was eliminated from the Morning Star Ceremony. A painting of Petalesharro, made when he visited Washington, D.C., to receive a medal for his bravery, now hangs in an art gallery in Tuscaloosa, Alabama.

This Stephen Seymour painting of a treaty council attended by Pawnees and U.S. soldiers in 1819 constitutes one of the earliest surviving visual documentations of a Pawnee-white encounter made by an actual participant.

When white trappers began to invade the western mountains in the 1820s they realized that the land was actually a far cry from what Lewis and Clark had called "the Great American Desert." A trapper by the name of Jedediah Smith wound up in the area that is now Republic, Kansas, and wintered with the Pawnee there during 1825. When he returned, his descriptions hinted at inexhaustible supplies of game, timber, and land; this encouraged others to come.

The Pawnee at first agreed to allow these new settlers to pass through. They had already signed a peace treaty with the U.S. government to this effect in 1818. It was when the people lingered, forcibly taking the Pawnee land and its wealth, that real troubles began.

The dawn of the Industrial Revolution was the beginning of the Pawnee's darkest night. European technological advances made themselves apparent in Pawnee lands. By the mid–19th century, telegraph lines spread across the Plains like a great spiderweb. The white man began to survey and lay track upon which the iron horse would travel. No formal treaties were signed establishing the railroads' right-of-way. Some of the lands the tracks crossed were those of the Pawnee, and Native American anxiety began to turn to outright rancor against the alien invaders.

On one morning in 1842, one hundred settlers in 18 covered wagons left Independence, Missouri, and began the first crossing of the Plains by settlers. The next year and every year after that the trickle of wagons increased to tidal wave proportions.

In the earliest days of the invasion into and through what was then called Indian country, some settlers were rather dismayed to cross the entire continent without having spotted an Indian. Many of the wagon trains of

the 1840s only saw Indians when they went by trading posts or forts along the way. By 1847, there were three main trails leading to the Far West: the Santa Fe, Oregon, and Mormon trails. The Santa Fe Trail was first worn down by the travois, having had its beginnings as a trading and hunting route. The Mormon Trail was begun by the followers of Brigham Young, who led

Albert Bierstadt's 1869 painting entitled The Oregon Trail *was one of many such works from the period to depict the landscape of the West in romantically grand, even heroic, terms. Artistic merit aside, such paintings helped encourage westward emigration. The Oregon Trail was one of several widely traveled ways west that traversed Pawnee territory.*

his people to what is now Salt Lake City, Utah. In addition to the three major trails, the Missouri River, fed by the Platte, provided transportation for traders and settlers via steamboat.

The discovery of gold in California in 1848 started a great transcontinental migration of miners, settlers, and others wanting to take advantage of the booming economy to be found in the

West. The following year, wagons rolled across the Plains as far as the eye could see. Along the Platte, where much of this activity occurred, buffalo became more wary. They avoided the noisy throngs of progress, eventually dividing themselves into two herds on the north and south sides of the river.

It was inevitable that the two cultures would clash. Settlers and other non-Indians held one of two opinions about Native Americans, both of which had their roots in paternalistic European attitudes. One belief was that the Indian was a proud, simple "child of nature," unencumbered by civilization and its immorality. The other view held that Indians were treacherous, bloodthirsty savages whose removal was necessary for the safety of the civilized world.

Both views were skewed. The policies of the U.S. government toward America's native inhabitants were equally misguided. The establishment of a special organization to handle Indian affairs did little to improve the situation. Originally part of the Department of the Interior, the Bureau of Indian Affairs was established by the

A pioneer family pauses in Nebraska's Loup Valley beside the "prairie schooner" on which it is making its way west. For the Pawnee, as for other Native American peoples, white settlement on their homelands meant conflict and an end to much of their traditional way of life.

For many of the new settlers in Nebraska, the reality of life on the prairie was somewhat less glamorous than depicted by Bierstadt and others.

U.S. government in 1824. Its original purpose was "to safeguard the welfare of American Indians . . . act as trustee for tribal lands and funds, supervise the reservations and provide welfare and education facilities." None of this, however, did the Native Americans really want or need.

The great overland migration of the 19th century brought more than people into Pawnee territory; white settlers and traders brought with them terrible diseases to which the Pawnee

had no natural immunities. In 1831, the Pawnee were hit with their first major epidemic brought by white settlers. Smallpox, an infectious disease causing fever, headache, and festering sores, killed more than half the Pawnee population. In 1849, cholera, a water-borne bacterial disease, became an epidemic and killed nearly half of what remained of the Pawnee population. The symptoms of cholera came on quickly, with severe diarrhea, dehydration, shock, and then death. The

After the completion of the transcontinental railroad in 1869, telegraph and then telephone wires soon followed the tracks west, resulting in further incursions onto Pawnee land.

survivors were so frightened of cholera that they often refused to bury the dead. Measles and tuberculosis also swept through the tribes, leaving death in their wake.

So weakened and dispirited were the Pawnee that by 1859, when they were ordered by the U.S. government to move to a reservation beside the Loup River near what is now Genoa,

Nebraska, they went without a fight. They found no peace there, however. The long-time enemy of the Pawnee, the Sioux, went unchecked by the government the Pawnee thought would protect them. Bands of Sioux raided Pawnee villages, killing even more of the people. In 1873, the Sioux attacked a Pawnee hunting band in a canyon near Trenton, Nebraska, killing almost everyone. A series of severe droughts killed the verdant grasses upon which the buffalo fed, causing the great herds to migrate farther in search of food. Grasshoppers, which darkened the Plains from horizon to horizon with their great numbers, destroyed what was left of the Pawnee's crops.

The Pawnee found themselves living a nightmare from which they could not awaken. In 1876, they were forced to cede their Nebraska reservation, their traditional hunting grounds, to the American government and migrate to Oklahoma.

As late as the 1800s, the great herds of buffalo upon which the Pawnee depended were without number. Estimates of the buffalo population by early explorers ranged from 20 to 60 million; one account mentions a horseback rider who traveled from sunrise to sunset through the same herd. There were several factors that led to the demise of the buffalo. Hunters and fur traders, the railroad, ranchers, and other settlers all played their parts in the extermination of the bison.

Certain parts of the buffalo, such as the tongue, were considered delicacies in Europe; the meat of the female buffalo was especially tender. Hunters began the wanton slaughter of the bison to supply this new demand. Because they mostly killed the cows, the numbers of newborn buffalo calves grew smaller every spring. The demand for hides skyrocketed when a German furrier developed a tanning method to make buffalo hide extreme-

ly soft. As a result, an increasing number of fur traders sought their fortunes on the Plains.

The results were tragically predictable. Pawnee hunting parties would come upon dead buffalo left to rot in the sun, with only the tongues, humps, and hides removed. Starvation began to be the rule rather than the exception in Pawnee life. The railroad also caused problems for the buffalo population. Settlers shot at the herds from their train cars just to watch the great beasts stagger and fall. It became a sport, something to pass the time while crossing the Plains.

By 1878, the southern herd was wiped out except for a few small, isolated herds. The northern herd, whose migration route was cut off by ranchers who had begun to use barbed wire in 1874, succumbed to the rifles of the huntsmen shortly thereafter. The symbol of Pawnee freedom and culture was disappearing before their eyes. Then came what seemed to be a chance to better themselves and perhaps change their destiny.

Across the Plains, the Sioux were playing havoc with the U.S. government's plans to settle the country. Forgetful that they themselves had caused the insurrection by reneging on treaties, the government decided to put down the massive Sioux uprising. They asked the Pawnee to help.

In 1864 the Civil War was still raging, and the Sioux were taking advantage of the fact that Union troops were busy fighting the Confederacy. There was little help for the settlers and other whites who roamed the Plains. After losing thousands of lives and after futile attempts to control the Sioux through normal governmental controls, about 200 Pawnee were made U.S. Army scouts, to serve in the Sioux Campaign of 1864 under Major Frank North and his brother, Captain Luther North.

The Pawnee must have seen this as an opportunity for revenge upon the Sioux Nation. Recent attacks by the Sioux, such as the bloody encounter at Trenton Canyon, were still fresh in Pawnee minds. To serve the new government with compensation *and* to strike a blow against their longtime enemies seemed a golden opportunity. In what is now termed "the Sioux Campaign," the company of Pawnee scouts served beside regular army troops and fought with dauntless courage. Major North became so pop-

Hunters sit atop a huge mound of 200,000 buffalo hides awaiting processing and shipment east in Dodge City, Kansas, in 1874. The eradication of the buffalo was a conscious strategy pursued by the U.S. government as a means of ending Indian resistance in the West.

ular with the Pawnee scouts that they came to call him *Pani Leshar*, which means "Pawnee Chief."

The scouts did so well in the Sioux Campaign that in 1867 they were again asked to aid the U.S. government by protecting construction workers on the Union Pacific Railroad. The completion of the first transcontinental railroad would unite the country, and Pawnee involvement in protecting the railroad was a terrible irony, for the iron horse brought more settlers to the Plains, helping to seal the fate of the Pawnee and other tribes.

The Pawnee were chosen for this particular duty because the U.S. Army, most notably the soldiers of Fort Sedgwick, could not outfight the raiding war parties of the other tribes, all of whom were enemies of the Pawnee Nation. Since 1863, these war parties, comprised of Sioux, Cheyenne, and Arapaho warriors, had been attacking the Union Pacific tracklayers and surveyors, taking lives, horses, and scalps. Colonel William Emory, the commander of Fort Sedgwick, was steadfastly opposed to "putting Cavalry uniforms on 200 half-wild Indians" and was offended that his superiors made this decision against his advice (he later admitted his error).

Of all the interesting stories concerning this time in Pawnee history, one man's story stands out. A half-white, half-Pawnee man named James Murie was one of nine officers given charge of the 200-strong contingent of scouts. Murie was made a captain of

Elvira Gaston Platt was a Protestant missionary to the Pawnee in Nebraska after the Civil War.

the cavalry because of his previous experience when, as second lieutenant, he led Pawnee scouts against the Sioux in what is now called the Powder River Expedition. He was given command of one of four companies in the new regrouped battalion.

James Murie had been raised by Pawnee foster parents on the reservation near Genoa, Nebraska. Perhaps

These four Pawnee scouts were photographed in 1869. Making use of the traditional enmity between the Pawnee and the Sioux, the U.S. Army employed Pawnee warriors as scouts to aid them in crushing the Sioux resistance and protecting the transcontinental railroad.

one reason he accepted the assignment to protect the Union Pacific was because of a renegade Cheyenne named Turkey Leg. Not only were his Cheyenne bands harassing the Union Pacific tracklayers, Turkey Leg had also led a raid on the Genoa reservation in 1865, killing Murie's foster parents.

The battalion was first issued Enfield rifles, then the more modern Spencer repeating rifles, which held seven rounds of ammunition in a tubular magazine and an eighth round in the chamber. The Spencers had a range of about 600 yards. The scouts carried the Spencers in a carbine sling, which allowed the rifle to hang by the right hip, muzzle down, when not in use, leaving the hands free.

The four companies were each assigned specific duties. One company guarded the survey crew; another the grading camp; a third the horse and mule herds. Murie's B Company was in charge of guarding the construction camp and the tracklayers. After the companies were in place, tracklayers were attacked by a band of about 80 Sioux led by Red Cloud. The Sioux were ambushed by Murie's B Company before they got within range of the tracklayers. The next attack was by the Cheyenne, led by Turkey Leg himself. Murie's 40 Pawnees again repelled the raiders. Murie and his battalion of Pawnee scouts helped to ensure peace long enough for the railroad to be completed.

The part the Pawnees played in helping white settlers establish roots in the West did little for them as a nation. The laws of the U.S. government would suppress them and all other Indian nations without regard. In the end, all "red men" were treated in the same disgraceful way, whether they had been ally, guide, warrior, or scout in their previous dealings with the white man.

In the first half of the 19th century, the Pawnee had been on generally peaceful terms with the American government. After that, however, American policy toward Native Americans in general seemed bent on assimilating the cultures and annihilating the histories of those who were here before.

The Major Crimes Act, passed in 1885, dealt with the question of Native Americans who committed crimes against one another. The act provided that any Native American accused of a "major" crime, such as murder, came under the jurisdiction of the U.S. government. Without the consent of the Indian nations, their own judicial systems were rendered powerless.

Congress passed the Dawes Act in 1887 to help Native Americans in the "assimilation" process. Named after its sponsor, Massachusetts senator Henry L. Dawes, this act was also called the General Allotment Act, and served a twofold purpose. Dawes reasoned that Native Americans would be better able to fit in with mainstream American culture if they owned land. The act allocated parcels of the existing reservations to individual male Native Americans; this was later changed to include females. The amount of land allotted depended upon one's age, marital status, and family condition (orphans under the age of 18 received twice the land of children living with their parents, for example).

If Native Americans were given American citizenship and turned into landholders, they could also be taxed.

To remove this burden, at least temporarily, Dawes included a 25-year period in which the U.S. government would hold the allotted lands "in trust" for the allottees. This period ostensibly would allow Native Americans time to make a profit from farming the land. They could also move away and live in cities with non–Native Americans and learn how to make a living like the "average" American. The act provided for education and farming instruction toward these ends.

What white Americans failed to realize was that most Native Americans did not wish to learn farming the white man's way. In any case, much of

James R. Murie (center, seated) was made a captain in the U.S. cavalry, with command responsibility for the Pawnee scouts. Photographed with Murie on this occasion were the Pawnee scouts Captain Jim and Billy Osborne (flanking Murie in front row) and John Buffalo, John Box, High Eagle, and Seeing Eagle (standing left to right at rear).

Pawnee children at the reservation school at the agency on the Loup River in 1871. With good reason the Pawnee, like other Native American tribes, would come to regard the education given to them at such reservation schools as an agent of cultural destruction.

the land given them for cultivation was barren wasteland. And when the act broke up reserved lands and gave Native Americans ownership of individual allotments, unscrupulous speculators could cajole individual Indians into selling their plots. Over time, the reservations would be eaten away piecemeal, and the land would be lost forever.

In their ignorance or greed, lawmakers, politicians, settlers, and others concerned with "the Indian problem" praised Dawes for his genius. They saw his act as the perfect solution, which would "settle" the Indians once and for all. The act, however, completely destroyed the sovereignty of the Native American nations over their own people. Thanks to the Dawes Act,

On the Pawnee agency in Nance County, Nebraska, near the town of Genoa, tipis and earth lodges stand in the foreground in front of the agency building. Against ever greater difficulties, the tribe tried to maintain as much of its traditional way of life as possible.

Native Americans found themselves owning less land than they had been allocated in the reservation treaties. The remainder found its way into the hands of white settlers, and appeals to tribal courts meant nothing.

Native Americans were further humiliated as they began to lose their sense of belonging to a tribe. For seven centuries or more, Pawnee culture had as its cornerstone an attitude of interdependence, of belonging to each other. With each individual owning land, and with their communal properties dissolved, what had been the backbone of their social structure simply vanished.

After the Pawnee had lost virtually all their lands, another piece of legislation caused them to suffer even further. The Curtis Act of 1898 effectively abolished the rights of all tribal governments. They were completely without power to rule, advise, educate, or lead their people, figuratively or otherwise. The people were completely and solely under the authority of the U.S. government.

Following the Curtis Act, in an effort to further "assimilate" or "Americanize" the Native American populations, Indian children were removed from their homes, often forcibly, and sent to school to learn the white man's ways. After 1875, the Pawnee Industrial School was constructed near the Pawnee Indian Agency just outside Pawnee, Oklahoma. There, children were taught the white man's language, ways, and beliefs. If a Pawnee child

By 1904, for most Americans the Pawnee existed more as a historical curiosity than as a living people. This Pawnee earth lodge and summer house were constructed as part of an exhibit at the 1904 World's Fair in St. Louis, Missouri.

A group of Pawnee wait on the platform at the St. Louis World's Fair for the train that will take them back to the reservation. Pawnees, as well as other Native Americans, enacted historical scenes as part of the World's Fair exhibits on Indian life.

were caught doing anything reminiscent of the "old ways," he was sometimes severely punished. It took over three decades before the Curtis Act was invalidated.

The Indian Reorganization Act of 1934, also known as the Wheeler-Howard Act after the two legislators who initiated the bill, was called the Indian New Deal, and represented a turning point in federal Indian policy. Bureau of Indian Affairs commissioner John Collier, whose efforts had inspired the legislation, was a man of unusual vision and a sense of fairness. During his tenure with the Bureau of

Indian Affairs, he initiated sweeping reforms in Indian policies.

The Indian Reorganization Act had three basic tenets. The first one rescinded Dawes's allotment provisions, returning to the nations all lands not already sold to whites. Instead of the 25-year trust agreement that Dawes had provided, the new act extended the trust period on allotments indefinitely. Collier had seen that when the 25-year trust period ended, many Native Americans could still not pay the new taxes on their allotted lands and were forced to sell them, often to whites. This extension of the trust period thus protected the allottees and their lands.

The Indian Reorganization Act also set aside $2 million annually for the purpose of buying back lands previously sold to whites and returning them to the previous owners. There were also provisions for tribal reorganization, allowing the nations limited self-government similar to that of municipalities.

A third tenet in the Indian Reorganization Act held that qualified Native Americans would be appointed to various offices within the Bureau of Indian Affairs itself. Young, promising Indian students would be provided with loans for education from a $250,000 annual fund set aside for this purpose.

Originally, Congress passed the bill with the stipulation that Native American tribes in Oklahoma and Alaska be excluded; they reasoned that these tribes, the Pawnee among them, did not need the protection this legislation provided. But because of Collier's persistence, in 1936 Congress passed the Oklahoma Indian Welfare Act, which extended many provisions of the Indian Reorganization Act to Native Americans on reservations there. Congress also founded the Indian Arts and Crafts Board to improve the economic conditions of Native Americans by helping them showcase and sell native handicrafts.

The 20th century has seen further improvements in U.S. federal policy as it relates to the Pawnee. In 1957, reservation lands that had not been given to white settlers in Oklahoma were returned to the Pawnee people. In 1968, the Pawnee Nation regained ownership of their Oklahoma Tribal Reservation, which the U.S. government had granted them in an earlier treaty in exchange for their Nebraska hunting grounds.

A Pawnee couple, Sara (St. Clair) Robinson and Charles Gover, lead a group of dancers in an Indian two-step. The Pawnee Nation is once again strong and vibrant, after nearing extinction in the early 20th century.

THE PAWNEE NATION TODAY

4

Today, a growing, progressive community exists on the 650-acre Pawnee Reserve just outside the city of Pawnee in northeastern Oklahoma. From a nation that was almost wiped out, the tribe has grown to include nearly 2,500 members in 1994.

The Pawnee are now able to practice many of the rites and traditions nearly lost to them. But it was inevitable that the Pawnee would be affected by their exposure to other cultures. For example, serving in the U.S. military, many of the young were introduced to new ways of thinking and decided against returning to the reservation, thinking that there was a better life for them elsewhere. Since the 1970s, however, there has been a renewed interest in the old ways and a longing for the sense of community that the people once shared.

The Pawnee Indian tribe of Oklahoma first ratified their Constitution in 1938, following passage of the Oklahoma Indian Welfare Act of 1936. The constitution was amended in 1982. The tribal government is made up of the eight-member Pawnee Tribal Business Council, the superior governing body. Council members are elected every two years in a general tribal election. Various subcommittees appointed by the tribal council include an education committee, a committee on aging, and a health board.

The other governing body is the Nasharo Council, also known as the Chief Council. Rather than being ruled by one chief, the Nasharo Council comprises eight traditional chiefs, with two chiefs representing each of the four bands.

The Pawnee flag symbolizes their history and regained cultural pride. The field has a blue background with miniature stars and stripes, representing America. In the center is the head

The Pawnee Tribal Business Council, past and present: Members of the 1939 council and the 1995 council (facing page) pose for photographs. The eight-member council has been the superior governing body of the tribe for over 50 years.

of a wolf (many of the Plains tribes called the Pawnees "wolves" because of their courage and cunning). Underneath the wolf's head are six arrowheads. They symbolize the six wars in which the Pawnee served—the Indian Wars, the Spanish-American War, the two world wars, the Korean War, and the Vietnam War.

The staff of the flag is a real warrior's lance, complete with flint spearhead. The staff is decorated with beadwork mounted on buckskin. The beads are multicolored, symbolizing those who have gone before. At the top of the flag are four eagle feathers, representing the four Pawnee bands. Because cedar is a sacred token of prayer and peace, on special occasions a sprig is attached to the top of the Pawnee flagstaff.

On the reservation, the Bureau of Indian Affairs and the Tribal Administration and Programs offices

are housed in what used to be the boarding school. There is a community building, a tribal trading post, and the Health and Community Services Department. The trading post sells what you might normally find in a small grocery, as well as Native American handicrafts.

Modeled after the traditional earth lodge, the roundhouse is used by the Pawnee community for special tribal functions. Like many other nations, the Pawnee have a bingo enterprise, located in the Roam Chief Community Recreation Center. There are a variety of churches both on and off the reservation. The Methodist, Baptist, and Native American churches are represented, among others.

The Pawnee people wear traditional clothing at tribal dances and pow-wows. Otherwise, their dress is much the same as that of any other American. Their diet consists of what you might eat every day, as well as some traditional foods such as corn soup, buffalo meat, blue corn mush, and fried bread.

The future for the Pawnee people is perhaps brighter now than it has been since the coming of the white man. True, if one were to focus only on the negative aspects, it would seem that alcoholism, suicide, poverty, and a

Charles W. Chapman's Kindred Spirits *(1989) celebrates traditional Pawnee identity and spirituality.*

lack of opportunities are the over-whelming facts of reservation life. But these are people with vision and ambi-tion, as were their ancestors before them. The Pawnee are working to change their lot, for the present and the future.

The Health and Community Ser-

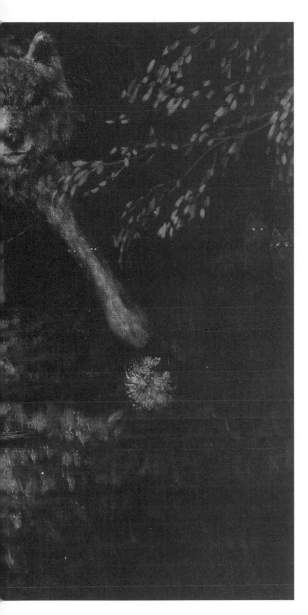

To care for the elderly who are unable to cook for or feed themselves, the Elderly Feeding Program was developed. The tribe also runs the Indian Children Welfare Program, which is supported by funds from the Pawnee and by volunteer efforts.

To ease the problems of poverty, the Health and Community Services Department has begun several programs to help with the costs of running a home, as well as a program that provides emergency shelter, support, training, and education services to victims of family violence.

Another unique problem that Native Americans have is the struggle for their ancestors' remains. Renewed pride in their heritage has encouraged the Pawnee to try to reclaim their ancestors, the remains of which are currently on display in museums and private collections both here and abroad. Many of these were dug by "treasure hunters" making their fortunes through modern-day grave robbing. The Pawnee Tribal Business Council has set up a reburial committee, which, as the name implies, properly buries the recovered remains of the long dead. Many artifacts, too, which are traded or are in public or private collections are liable for such repatriation.

The door to the future is wide open for Pawnee children. Area schools have an Indian education coordinator who has established special tutorial programs to enhance not only higher education but also cultural awareness

vices Department has established special programs aimed at dealing with depression and suicide. The Substance Abuse Program provides prevention activities, counseling, and aftercare to individuals and their affected families.

for Pawnee students. Under this program, the Pawnee language is being reinstituted in the form of computerized language courses, open to all interested students. All Pawnee students showing promise are eligible for funds to attend college or to get vocational training. Many tribal members have become attorneys, doctors, nurses, teachers, and other professionals.

Public tours of the Pawnee Reserve are currently in the planning stages, but children from nearby schools often visit and attend dances and ceremonies held at the tribal campgrounds. There are two museums of note that seek to preserve the memory of a people who once freely roamed the plains and called it home. In Courtland, Kansas, lies the Pawnee Indian Village Museum. It was built in the shape of an earth lodge. The site near the Republican River was the natural choice; an ancient grouping of earth lodges was uncovered there during the 1900s. State historians, anthropologists, and archaeologists all agree that this was the place where Jedediah Smith, the trapper, wintered with the Pawnee in 1824.

South of Anadarko, Oklahoma, Indian City USA has exhibits depicting the life of the Pawnee and six other tribes. There is also a rather large buffalo herd on adjoining acreage, and Native American dances and pow-wows are held throughout the year.

For the people of the Pawnee nation, perhaps the greatest challenge for preserving their culture lies within

themselves. In a world that denigrates the unique and places greater value on cultural assimilation, they must strive to maintain their spiritual integrity and cultural heritage.

More than a few Pawnee have brought honor to themselves and their people with their special talents.

Dancers perform at the 49th annual Pawnee Indian Homecoming and Powwow, held in 1995. Dances and powwows not only attract tourist dollars but give tribal members an opportunity to celebrate their heritage.

Brummett EchoHawk, a writer and artist living in Tulsa, Oklahoma, designed the flag for the nation. His nephew, Larry EchoHawk, is the attor- ney general of Idaho and at this time is running for governor of the state. Writer Anna Lee Walters has published many stories of Pawnee life, preserv-

Alexander Mathews (left), a veteran of World War II, carries the U.S. flag while Merton Moore, who served in the Korean War, carries the Pawnee war veterans' flag in this 1995 photograph.

ing in print what otherwise might have been lost forever. She is also the director of the Navajo Community Press in Tsaile, Arizona.

In 1946, the tribe first gathered to celebrate the returning Pawnee veterans of World War II. This has since become an annual event. The Pawnee Indian Homecoming, or powwow, is now a four-day event, held around the first weekend in July at the Pawnee Fairgrounds. Here participants enjoy traditional foods, dancing, various contests, softball games, and a parade. There is also a five-mile endurance race, named after Hawk Chief, a Pawnee scout who was the first person to run a mile in under four minutes. He first set this record in the mid-1870s. It remained unbroken for nearly a hundred years, until in 1954 an Englishman, Roger Bannister, ran the mile in 3:59.4.

In many ways the city of Pawnee celebrates its link with the tribe. It is the home of Pawnee Bill's Wild West

President Bill Clinton greets Native American performers in 1993. Clinton has promised to give the various tribes a greater voice in federal Indian policy.

Show, which entertains tourists with Native American warriors and dancers. A museum with artifacts of the "Old West," as well as endless parades and celebrations, are all reminders of the connection the town has with Pawnee culture.

On April 29, 1994, President Bill Clinton held the first Native American summit since 1822. He pledged "to respect tribal governments and improve relations between [his] administration and the Indians." He promised to "heal the pain" of the nations in various ways, one of which will be to consult with them on future federal Indian policies. Although many Native Americans remain skeptical in light of similar overtures in the past, there is hope that at last the descendants of the people who were here before us will have a greater voice in governing their affairs.

Every civilization has periods of growth and decline. Perhaps after their long night in a valley of despair, the Pawnee will once again reach the mountaintop, where they will be close enough to touch the stars from whence they came.

BIBLIOGRAPHY

Andrist, Ralph K. *Long Death: The Last Days of the Plains Indians.* New York: Collier Books, 1964.

Capps, Benjamin. *The Great Chiefs.* Alexandria, VA: Time-Life Books, 1975.

Creigh, Dorothy Weyer. *Nebraska: A Bicentennial History.* New York: Norton, 1977.

Davis, Kenneth S. *Kansas: A Bicentennial History.* New York: Norton, 1976.

Erdoes, Richard, and Alfonso Ortiz. *American Indian Myths and Legends.* New York: Pantheon Books, 1984.

Fradin, Dennis B. *The Pawnee.* Chicago: Children's Press, 1988.

Hahn, Elizabeth. *The Pawnee.* Vero Beach, FL: Rourke, 1992.

Lankford, George E. *Native American Legends.* Little Rock, AR: August House, 1987.

McSpadden, J. Walker. *Indian Heroes.* New York: Thomas Y. Crowell, 1950.

Nathan, Adele. *The Building of the First Transcontinental Railroad.* New York: Random House, 1950.

Tassin, Ray. *Red Men in Blue.* Clinton, MA: Colonial Press, Inc., 1960.

Weltfish, Gene. *The Lost Universe: Pawnee Life and Culture.* Lincoln: University of Nebraska Press, 1977.

THE PAWNEE AT A GLANCE

TRIBE   *The Pawnee*
CULTURE AREA   *Great Plains*
GEOGRAPHY   *Present-day Kansas and Nebraska*
LINGUISTIC FAMILY   *Caddoan*
CURRENT POPULATION   *2,500*
FEDERAL STATUS   *Recognized; tribal reservation in northeastern Oklahoma*

GLOSSARY

band A loosely organized group of people who are bound together by the need for food and defense, by family ties, or by other common interests.

Bureau of Indian Affairs (BIA) A U.S. government agency within the Department of the Interior. Originally intended to manage trade and other relations with Indians, the BIA now seeks to develop and implement programs that encourage Indians to manage their own affairs and to improve their educational opportunities and general social and economic well-being.

Caddoans The ancestors of the Pawnee, who lived in the area immediately west of the Mississippi River.

cedar A type of pine tree that has especially fragrant and durable wood. Cedar is a sacred substance to the Pawnee.

counting coup Performing acts of valor during warfare; or, a system of ranking such acts.

Curtis Act A federal law that placed Native Americans completely under the control of the U.S. government, denying them the right to govern themselves.

Dawes Act Also known as the General Allotment Act, a federal law that divided tribal land holdings into small plots to be held as private property by individual Native Americans. The Dawes Act severely reduced the acreage held by Native Americans and undermined tribal traditions of communal land ownership.

earth lodge A large, round dwelling made of support poles covered with a mix of mud, grass, and rocks and occupied during the spring and fall.

Hunt Police A special society of Pawnee men who enforced certain rules surrounding the buffalo hunt that were designed to increase the hunt's success.

Indian Reorganization Act (IRA) The 1934 federal law that ended the policy of allotting plots of land to individuals and encouraged the development of reservation communities. The act also provided for the creation of autonomous tribal governments.

Major Crimes Act A federal law that placed any Native American who committed a serious crime under the jurisdiction of the U.S. court system, thereby undermining a tribe's ability to govern itself.

medicine bundle A collection of sacred objects contained in a special carrying case.

Among the Pawnee, certain bundles represent the creation, the four semi-cardinal directions, and intellectual creativity.

Morning Star Ceremony A traditional Pawnee religious ceremony performed in the spring that involved the sacrifice of an adolescent girl from an enemy tribe.

shaman A holy man, also known as a priest or medicine man, who advised the tribe and performed protective rites.

Sioux A confederation of tribes that inhabit the northern Great Plains. The Sioux were traditionally considered enemies of the Pawnee.

sweat lodge A special lodge that was heated and filled with steam for baths and purification rituals.

INDEX

PICTURE CREDITS

THERESA JENSEN LACEY, an award-winning freelance writer and journalist, has been accepted to the 1995 *Who's Who in the South and Southwest*. A descendant of Chief Quanah Parker, she was inspired by her Comanche and Cherokee lineage to study Native American history. Lacey, who also wrote *The Blackfeet*, currently lives in Tennessee.

FRANK W. PORTER III, general editor of INDIANS OF NORTH AMERICA, is director of the Chelsea House Foundation for American Indian Studies. He holds a B.A., M.A., and Ph.D. from the University of Maryland. He has done extensive research concerning the Indians of Maryland and Delaware and is the author of numerous articles on their history, archaeology, geography, and ethnography. He was formerly director of the Maryland Commission on Indian Affairs and the American Indian Research and Resource Institute, Gettysburg, Pennsylvania, and he has received grants from the Delaware Humanities Forum, the Maryland Committee for the Humanities, the Ford Foundation, and the National Endowment for the Humanities, among others. Dr. Porter is the author of *The Bureau of Indian Affairs* in the Chelsea House KNOW YOUR GOVERNMENT series.